HMH SOCIAL STUDIES

W9-AGE-597

EASTERN WORLD
GEOGRAPHY

Guided Reading Workbook

chap 3. leson 1 PG 47
Leson 3 ⌐ ⌐ ⌐ ⌐ 2 PG 51
Leson 4 PG 55 PG 58

Contents

How to Use This Book

The *Guided Reading Workbook* was developed to help you get the most from your reading. Using this workbook alongside your textbook will help you master geography content while developing your reading and vocabulary skills. Reviewing the next few pages before getting started will make you aware of the many useful features in this book.

Lesson summary pages allow you to interact with the content and key terms and places from each section of a module. The summaries explain each section of your textbook in a way that is easy to understand.

Lesson numbers make it easy to find your place in the workbook.

The main idea statements help focus your attention as you read the summaries.

Definitions for the key terms and places from your textbook are given.

Headings under each lesson summary match those of your textbook, which can help you find the material you need.

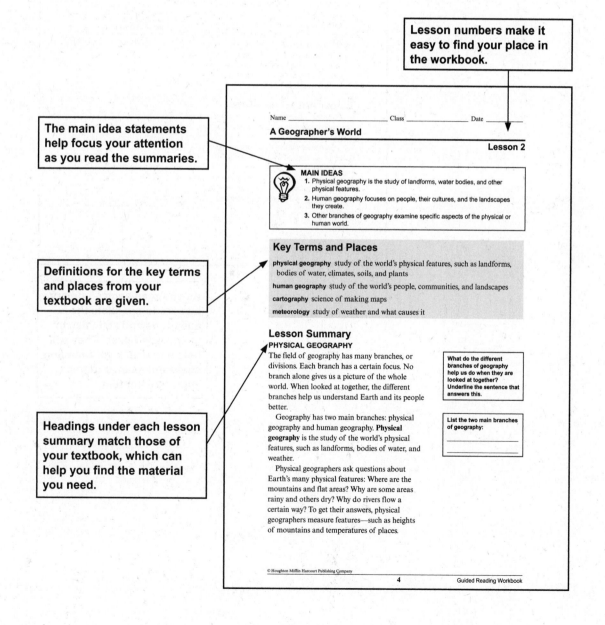

Name _____ Class _____ Date _____

A Geographer's World

Lesson 2

MAIN IDEAS
1. Physical geography is the study of landforms, water bodies, and other physical features.
2. Human geography focuses on people, their cultures, and the landscapes they create.
3. Other branches of geography examine specific aspects of the physical or human world.

Key Terms and Places

physical geography study of the world's physical features, such as landforms, bodies of water, climates, soils, and plants

human geography study of the world's people, communities, and landscapes

cartography science of making maps

meteorology study of weather and what causes it

Lesson Summary
PHYSICAL GEOGRAPHY
The field of geography has many branches, or divisions. Each branch has a certain focus. No branch alone gives us a picture of the whole world. When looked at together, the different branches help us understand Earth and its people better.

Geography has two main branches: physical geography and human geography. **Physical geography** is the study of the world's physical features, such as landforms, bodies of water, and weather.

Physical geographers ask questions about Earth's many physical features: Where are the mountains and flat areas? Why are some areas rainy and others dry? Why do rivers flow a certain way? To get their answers, physical geographers measure features—such as heights of mountains and temperatures of places.

What do the different branches of geography help us do when they are looked at together? Underline the sentence that answers this.

List the two main branches of geography:

_____

_____

© Houghton Mifflin Harcourt Publishing Company

4   Guided Reading Workbook

The key terms and places from your textbook have been boldfaced, allowing you to quickly find and study them.

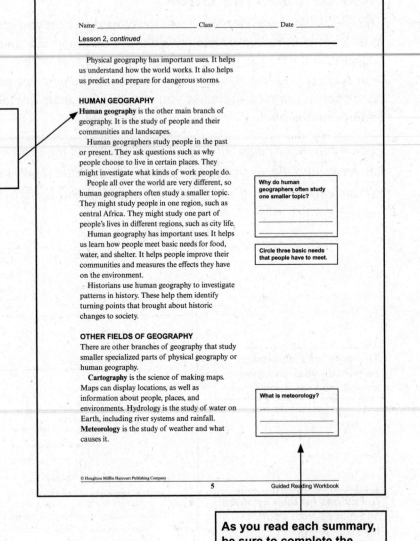

Name _____ Class _____ Date _____

Lesson 2, *continued*

Physical geography has important uses. It helps us understand how the world works. It also helps us predict and prepare for dangerous storms.

HUMAN GEOGRAPHY

Human geography is the other main branch of geography. It is the study of people and their communities and landscapes.

Human geographers study people in the past or present. They ask questions such as why people choose to live in certain places. They might investigate what kinds of work people do.

People all over the world are very different, so human geographers often study a smaller topic. They might study people in one region, such as central Africa. They might study one part of people's lives in different regions, such as city life.

Human geography has important uses. It helps us learn how people meet basic needs for food, water, and shelter. It helps people improve their communities and measures the effects they have on the environment.

Historians use human geography to investigate patterns in history. These help them identify turning points that brought about historic changes to society.

OTHER FIELDS OF GEOGRAPHY

There are other branches of geography that study smaller specialized parts of physical geography or human geography.

Cartography is the science of making maps. Maps can display locations, as well as information about people, places, and environments. Hydrology is the study of water on Earth, including river systems and rainfall. **Meteorology** is the study of weather and what causes it.

> Why do human geographers often study one smaller topic?
> _____
> _____
> _____

> Circle three basic needs that people have to meet.

> What is meteorology?
> _____
> _____
> _____

© Houghton Mifflin Harcourt Publishing Company

5   Guided Reading Workbook

As you read each summary, be sure to complete the questions and activities in the margin boxes. They will help you check your reading comprehension and track important content.

Each lesson has activities that allow you to demonstrate your understanding of the lesson's key terms and places. Use the lesson summaries and your textbook to answer these activities.

The challenge activity provides an opportunity for you to apply important critical thinking skills using the content that you learned in the lesson.

A variety of activities helps you check your knowledge of key terms and places.

Some pages have a word bank. You can use it to help find answers or complete writing activities.

Writing activities require you to include key words and places in what you write. Remember to check to make sure you are using the terms and places correctly.

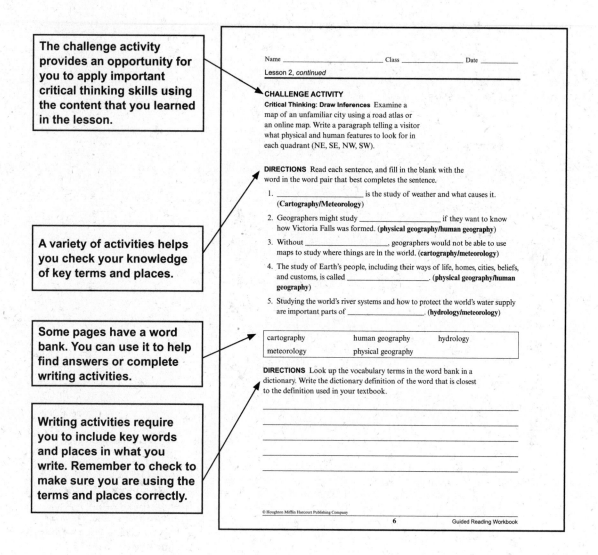

Name _____ Class _____ Date _____

Lesson 2, *continued*

CHALLENGE ACTIVITY

Critical Thinking: Draw Inferences Examine a map of an unfamiliar city using a road atlas or an online map. Write a paragraph telling a visitor what physical and human features to look for in each quadrant (NE, SE, NW, SW).

DIRECTIONS Read each sentence, and fill in the blank with the word in the word pair that best completes the sentence.

1. _____ is the study of weather and what causes it. (**Cartography/Meteorology**)

2. Geographers might study _____ if they want to know how Victoria Falls was formed. (**physical geography/human geography**)

3. Without _____, geographers would not be able to use maps to study where things are in the world. (**cartography/meteorology**)

4. The study of Earth's people, including their ways of life, homes, cities, beliefs, and customs, is called _____. (**physical geography/human geography**)

5. Studying the world's river systems and how to protect the world's water supply are important parts of _____. (**hydrology/meteorology**)

cartography	human geography	hydrology
meteorology	physical geography	

DIRECTIONS Look up the vocabulary terms in the word bank in a dictionary. Write the dictionary definition of the word that is closest to the definition used in your textbook.

_____
_____
_____
_____
_____

© Houghton Mifflin Harcourt Publishing Company

6   Guided Reading Workbook

A Geographer's World

MAIN IDEAS
1. Geography is the study of the world, its people, and the landscapes they create.
2. Geographers look at the world in many different ways.

Key Terms and Places

geography study of the world, its people, and the landscapes they create

landscape human and physical features that make a place unique

social science field that studies people and the relationships among them

region part of the world with one or more common features distinguishing it from surrounding areas

Lesson Summary
WHAT IS GEOGRAPHY?

For every place on Earth, you can ask questions to learn about it: What does the land look like? What is the weather like? What are people's lives like? Asking questions like these is how you study geography. **Geography** is the study of the world, its people, and the physical and human **landscapes** that make a place unique.

Geographers (people who study geography) ask questions about how the world works. For example, they may ask why a place gets tornadoes. To find answers, they gather data by observing and measuring. Then they study and interpret the data. In this way, geography is like science.

Geography can also be like a social science. **Social science** studies people and how they relate to each other. This information cannot be measured in the same way. To study people, geographers may visit places and talk to the people about their lives.

Underline the sentences that state how geography is like science.

LOOKING AT THE WORLD

Geographers must look carefully at the world around them. Depending on what they want to learn, they look at the world at different levels.

Geographers may study at the local level, such as a city or town. They may ask why people live there, what work they do, and how they travel. They can help a town or city plan improvements.

Geographers may also study at the regional level. A **region** is an area with common features. A region may be big or small. Its features make it different from areas around it. The features may be physical (such as mountains) or human (such as language).

Sometimes geographers study at the global level. They study how people interact all over the world. Geographers can help us learn how people's actions affect other people and places. For example, they may ask how one region influences other regions.

> Circle the three levels that geographers study.

CHALLENGE ACTIVITY

Critical Thinking: Evaluate Find a map of your state. Determine the state's different regions based on physical characteristics. Are there regions with mountains, ones near important bodies of water, regions that rely on farming, or areas with lots of cities? Make a list of the regions and each one's characteristics. Which region do you live in?

DIRECTIONS On the line provided before each statement, write **T** if the statement is true and **F** if the statement is false. If the statement is false, write the correct term on the line after each sentence that makes the sentence a true statement.

_____ 1. The study of the world, its people, and the landscapes they create is called <u>geography</u>.

_____

_____ 2. Geography is sometimes called a <u>social science</u> because it studies people and the relationships among them.

_____

_____ 3. An example of a small <u>region</u> that geographers might study is Chinatown in San Francisco.

_____

_____ 4. The combination of human and physical features that make a place unique is called a <u>landscape</u>.

_____

_____ 5. When geographers study how people live on a <u>global level</u>, they look at a single city or town.

_____

A Geographer's World

MAIN IDEAS
1. Physical geography is the study of landforms, water bodies, and other physical features.
2. Human geography focuses on people, their cultures, and the landscapes they create.
3. Other branches of geography examine specific aspects of the physical or human world.

Key Terms and Places

physical geography study of the world's physical features, such as landforms, bodies of water, climates, soils, and plants

human geography study of the world's people, communities, and landscapes

cartography science of making maps

meteorology study of weather and what causes it

Lesson Summary
PHYSICAL GEOGRAPHY

The field of geography has many branches, or divisions. Each branch has a certain focus. No branch alone gives us a picture of the whole world. When looked at together, the different branches help us understand Earth and its people better.

Geography has two main branches: physical geography and human geography. **Physical geography** is the study of the world's physical features, such as landforms, bodies of water, and weather.

Physical geographers ask questions about Earth's many physical features: Where are the mountains and flat areas? Why are some areas rainy and others dry? Why do rivers flow a certain way? To get their answers, physical geographers measure features—such as heights of mountains and temperatures of places.

What do the different branches of geography help us do when they are looked at together? Underline the sentence that answers this.

List the two main branches of geography:

_____

_____

Guided Reading Workbook

Physical geography has important uses. It helps us understand how the world works. It also helps us predict and prepare for dangerous storms.

HUMAN GEOGRAPHY

Human geography is the other main branch of geography. It is the study of people and their communities and landscapes.

Human geographers study people in the past or present. They ask questions such as why people choose to live in certain places. They might investigate what kinds of work people do.

People all over the world are very different, so human geographers often study a smaller topic. They might study people in one region, such as central Africa. They might study one part of people's lives in different regions, such as city life.

Human geography has important uses. It helps us learn how people meet basic needs for food, water, and shelter. It helps people improve their communities and measures the effects they have on the environment.

Historians use human geography to investigate patterns in history. These help them identify turning points that brought about historic changes to society.

OTHER FIELDS OF GEOGRAPHY

There are other branches of geography that study smaller specialized parts of physical geography or human geography.

Cartography is the science of making maps. Maps can display locations, as well as information about people, places, and environments. Hydrology is the study of water on Earth, including river systems and rainfall. **Meteorology** is the study of weather and what causes it.

> Why do human geographers often study one smaller topic?
> _____
> _____
> _____

> Circle three basic needs that people have to meet.

> What is meteorology?
> _____
> _____
> _____

CHALLENGE ACTIVITY
Critical Thinking: Draw Inferences Examine a
map of an unfamiliar city using a road atlas or
an online map. Write a paragraph telling a visitor
what physical and human features to look for in
each quadrant (NE, SE, NW, SW).

DIRECTIONS Read each sentence, and fill in the blank with the
word in the word pair that best completes the sentence.

1. _____ is the study of weather and what causes it.
   (**Cartography/Meteorology**)

2. Geographers might study _____ if they want to know
   how Victoria Falls was formed. (**physical geography/human geography**)

3. Without _____, geographers would not be able to use
   maps to study where things are in the world. (**cartography/meteorology**)

4. The study of Earth's people, including their ways of life, homes, cities, beliefs,
   and customs, is called _____. (**physical geography/human
   geography**)

5. Studying the world's river systems and how to protect the world's water supply
   are important parts of _____. (**hydrology/meteorology**)

cartography	human geography	hydrology
meteorology	physical geography	

DIRECTIONS Look up the vocabulary terms in the word bank in a
dictionary. Write the dictionary definition of the word that is closest
to the definition used in your textbook.

_____

_____

_____

_____

_____

Guided Reading Workbook

A Geographer's World

> **MAIN IDEAS**
> 1. The five themes of geography help us organize our studies of the world.
> 2. The six essential elements of geography highlight some of the subject's most important ideas.

Key Terms and Places

absolute location specific description of where a place is

relative location general description of where a place is

environment an area's land, water, climate, plants and animals, and other physical features

Lesson Summary
THE FIVE THEMES OF GEOGRAPHY

Geographers use themes in their work. A theme is a topic that is common throughout a discussion or event. Many holidays have a theme, such as the flag and patriotism on the Fourth of July.

There are five major themes of geography: Location, Place, Human-Environment Interaction, Movement, and Regions. Geographers can use these themes in almost everything they study.

Location describes where a place is. This may be specific, such as an address. This is called an **absolute location.** It may also be general, such as saying the United States is north of Central America. This is called a **relative location.**

Place refers to an area's landscape. The landscape is made up of the physical and human features of a place, such as the land, climate, or people. Together, these features give a place its own identity apart from other places.

Human-Environment Interaction studies how people and their environment affect each other. The **environment** includes an area's physical

> List the five major themes of geography:
> _____
> _____
> _____
> _____

features, such as land, water, weather, and animals. Geographers study how people change their environment (by building dams or towns, for example). They also study how the environment causes people to adapt (by dressing for the weather, for example).

Movement involves learning about why and how people move. Do they move for work or pleasure? Do they travel by roads or other routes?

Studying Regions helps geographers learn how places are alike and different. This also helps them learn why places developed the way they did.

> **Describe two ways that people and their environment affect each other.**
> _____
> _____
> _____
> _____

THE SIX ESSENTIAL ELEMENTS

It is important to organize how you study geography so you get the most complete picture of a place. Using the five major themes can help you do this. Using the six essential elements can, too.

Geographers and teachers created the six elements from 18 basic ideas, called standards. The standards say what everyone should understand about geography. Each element groups together the standards that are related to each other.

The six elements are The World in Spatial Terms (*spatial* refers to where places are located), Places and Regions, Physical Systems, Human Systems, Environment and Society, and Uses of Geography. The six elements build on the five themes, so some elements and themes are similar. Uses of Geography is not part of the five themes. It focuses on how people can use geography to learn about the past and present and plan for the future.

> **What do the five themes and six elements of geography help you do? Underline the sentence that explains this.**

CHALLENGE ACTIVITY

Critical Thinking: Analyze Analyze a place you regularly visit, such as a vacation spot or a park in your neighborhood. Write a question about the place for each geography theme to help someone not familiar with the themes to understand them.

DIRECTIONS Write a word or phrase that has the same meaning as the term given.

1. absolute location _____

_____

2. element _____

_____

3. environment _____

_____

4. interaction _____

_____

5. relative location _____

_____

| absolute location | element | environment |
| interaction | relative location | |

DIRECTIONS Choose at least four of the vocabulary words from the word bank. Use these words to write a story or poem that relates to the lesson.

_____

_____

_____

_____

_____

_____

_____

_____

_____

A Geographer's World

Lesson 4

MAIN IDEA

1. Maps and globes are the most commonly used tools of geographers.
2. Many geographers study information gathered by satellites.
3. Geographers use many other tools, including graphs, charts, databases, and models in their work.

Key Terms and Places

map flat drawing that shows part of Earth's surface

globe spherical model of the entire planet

Global Positioning System (GPS) tool that uses satellites to transmit locations of objects on Earth

Geographic Information System (GIS) information from many geographic data sources

Lesson Summary
MAPS AND GLOBES

Geographers need tools to do their work. Often, they use maps and globes. A **map** is a flat drawing that shows Earth's surface. A **globe** is a spherical (round) model of the whole planet.

Maps and globes both show what Earth looks like. Because a globe is round, it can show Earth as it really is. To show the round Earth on a flat map, some details have to change. For example, a place's shape may change a little. But maps have benefits. They are easier to work with. They can also show small areas, such as cities, better.

> Underline two sentences that tell the benefits of using maps.

SATELLITES

Geographers also use images and information from satellites. These images help geographers see what Earth looks like from far above.

Satellites are part of a **Global Positioning System (GPS).** This system uses 24 satellites to transmit information about locations of objects on Earth. Many people use GPS in their cars to find out how to get to a new place.

> Why do drivers use GPS in their cars?
>
> _____
>
> _____
>
> _____

Lesson 4, *continued*

OTHER GEOGRAPHIC TOOLS

Geographers use many other tools, including notebooks and voice recorders to take notes. They also work with computers, which lets them use a **Geographic Information System (GIS).** GIS makes it possible to get information from many data sources.

Geographers can ask GIS a question such as, "What are the most important geographic characteristics of an airport site?" GIS answers the question with different kinds of information, including maps.

> **Circle the tools geographers use to take notes.**

CHALLENGE ACTIVITY

Critical Thinking: Develop Pick a city you would like to study. You want to develop the most complete picture possible of this place and its people. Make a list of questions to ask and tools you would use to find the answers.

DIRECTIONS Circle the word or statement that relates most closely to the vocabulary word.

1. **globe:** spherical, city streets, drawing

2. **map:** entire planet, changed shapes, round

3. **Global Positioning System (GPS):** close-up images, satellites, regional languages

4. **Geographic Information System (GIS):** notebooks, driving directions, computer data

A Geographer's World

MAIN IDEAS

1. When creating maps, cartographers use a pattern of latitude and longitude lines that circle Earth.
2. Cartographers have created map projections to show the round surface of Earth on a flat piece of paper.
3. Cartographers provide features to help users read maps.
4. There are different kinds of maps for different uses.
5. There are many kinds of landforms and other features on Earth.

Key Terms and Places

grid imaginary lines that circle Earth in east–west and north–south directions

latitude east–west lines in the grid

parallels lines of latitude

longitude north–south lines in the grid

meridians lines of longitude

degrees units of measurement that locate lines of latitude and longitude

minutes unit of measurement that is 1/60 of a degree

equator imaginary line that circles the globe halfway between the North and South Poles

prime meridian imaginary line that divides the globe into east and west halves

hemispheres northern and southern or eastern and western halves of the globe

continents seven large landmasses on Earth's surface

map projections ways that our round planet can be shown on a flat map

Lesson Summary
LATITUDE AND LONGITUDE

Geographers created a pattern of imaginary lines that circle the globe. These lines are called a **grid.** East–west lines are lines of **latitude.** They are also called **parallels** because they are always parallel to each other. North–south lines are called lines of **longitude,** or **meridians.** They pass through the poles.

Why are lines of latitude called parallels?

_____

_____

Guided Reading Workbook

The location of latitude and longitude is measured using **degrees,** or a ° symbol. Degrees are divided into 60 smaller measurements called **minutes.** Degrees and minutes help geographers locate any place on Earth.

Lines of latitude are north and south of the equator. The **equator** is an imaginary line that circles the globe halfway between the North and South Poles. Lines of longitude are east and west of an imaginary line called the **prime meridian.** The prime meridian divides the globe into east and west halves.

Lines of latitude start at 0° at the equator. North of the equator, they are labeled with an *N.* For example, the North Pole is located at 90°N. South of the equator, they are labeled with an *S.* The South Pole is located at 90°S.

Lines of longitude start at 0° at the prime meridian. They go up to 180°, which is the middle of the Pacific Ocean. Meridians west of the prime meridian to 180° are labeled with a *W.* Meridians east of the prime meridian to 180° are labeled with an *E.*

The equator and prime meridian divide the globe into **hemispheres,** or halves. The equator divides the world into the Northern Hemisphere and Southern Hemisphere. The prime meridian divides it into the Eastern Hemisphere and Western Hemisphere.

Earth's surface is further divided into seven large landmasses, called **continents.** Earth's major ocean region is divided into five smaller oceans.

> **Underline the sentence that states how degree measurements help geographers.**

> **What are the latitudes of the most northern and most southern points on Earth?**
> _____
> _____

> **Circle the imaginary line that divides the globe into Northern and Southern Hemispheres.**

MAP PROJECTIONS

Mapmakers use **map projections** to show our round planet on a flat map. All flat maps are distorted in some way. Mapmakers use one of three map projections: cylindrical, conic, or flat-plane.

Cylindrical projections are based on a cylinder wrapped around a globe at the equator. These maps pull the meridians apart so they are parallel to each other and do not meet at the poles. This makes the land areas at the poles look larger.

Conic projections are based on a cone placed over a globe. It is most accurate along the lines of latitude where the cone touches the globe.

Flat-plane projections are based on a flat shape touching the globe at only one point, such as the North Pole. It shows true direction and true area. That can help navigators. However, it distorts the shapes of land areas.

> Circle the three types of map projections.

> Underline the sentence that explains why navigators might want to use a flat-planed map.

MAP FEATURES

Most maps include four features that help us understand them and what they present. The first feature we usually see is a title. The map title tells you what the map is trying to show. Another feature is a compass rose. This has arrows that show which way north, south, east, and west lie on the map. A third feature is a scale. It is used to measure the distance between points on a map. The fourth important feature is a legend. It explains what symbols and colors represent on the map. For example, roads might be different colors, showing whether they are highways or two lanes.

Some maps include a locator map as a fifth feature. This shows where the area on the map is located in the larger world.

> Circle the four features you are likely to find on most maps.

Guided Reading Workbook

DIFFERENT KINDS OF MAPS

Political and physical maps are two of the most common maps, but there are also many types of thematic maps. Political maps use different colors to show borders of countries, capital cities, and other places in a region. Physical maps show features like mountain ranges, rivers, and deserts in a region. They often use different colors to represent different elevations. Thematic maps focus on one topic, like climate, resources, or population. They may show the information using different colors, arrows, or other symbols.

Name three kinds of thematic maps.
_____
_____
_____

EARTH'S SURFACE FEATURES

Landforms are features on Earth's surface that are formed by nature. There are many kinds of landforms and water features on Earth. Landform features include hills, valleys, and mountains, while water features include oceans, rivers, and lakes.

CHALLENGE ACTIVITY

Critical Thinking: Design a Map Create a small map of your school. Add a title, compass rose, scale, and legend to explain what the map is about and how to understand its colors and symbols.

DIRECTIONS On the line provided before each statement, write **T** if the statement is true and **F** if the statement is false. If the statement is false, write the correct answer on the line after each sentence that makes the sentence a true statement.

_____ 1. Lines of <u>longitude</u> are also called <u>meridians</u>.

_____

_____ 2. Geographers created a <u>grid</u> to help find locations on the globe.

_____

_____ 3. <u>Minutes</u> are divided in smaller units called <u>degrees</u>.

_____

_____ 4. Lines of <u>latitude</u> meet at the poles.

_____

_____ 5. The <u>equator</u> divides the globe into a Northern <u>Hemisphere</u> and a Southern Hemisphere.

_____

_____ 6. The location of the <u>prime meridian</u> is 0°.

_____

_____ 7. Lines of <u>latitude</u> run in parallel east–west paths around the globe.

_____

_____ 8. Mapmakers use a <u>compass rose</u> to show our round planet on a flat map.

_____

_____ 9. The seven large landmasses on Earth's surface are called <u>continents</u>.

_____

Guided Reading Workbook

The Physical World

MAIN IDEAS
1. Earth's movement affects the amount of energy we receive from the sun.
2. Earth's seasons are caused by the planet's tilt.

Key Terms and Places

solar energy energy from the sun

rotation one complete spin of Earth on its axis

revolution one trip of Earth around the sun

tropics regions close to the equator

Lesson Summary
EARTH'S MOVEMENT

Energy from the sun, or **solar energy,** is necessary for life on Earth. It helps plants grow and provides light and heat. Several factors affect the amount of solar energy Earth receives. These are rotation, revolution, tilt, and latitude.

> List the four factors that affect the amount of solar energy Earth receives.
> _____
> _____

Earth's axis is an imaginary rod running from the North Pole to the South Pole. Earth spins around on its axis. One complete **rotation** takes 24 hours, or one day. It looks as if the sun is moving, but it is really the planet's rotation that creates that effect.

Solar energy reaches only half of the planet at a time. The half that faces the sun receives light and warmth, creating daytime. In the half that faces away from the sun, it is nighttime, which is darker and cooler.

> What would happen if Earth did not rotate?
> _____
> _____
> _____

As Earth rotates, it also moves around the sun. It takes Earth a year, 365 1/4 days, to complete one **revolution** around the sun. Every four years, an extra day is added to February. This makes up for the extra quarter of a day.

> Underline the sentence that describes Earth's revolution around the sun.

Earth's axis is tilted, not straight up and down. At different times of year, some locations tilt toward

the sun. They get more solar energy than
locations tilted away from the sun.

Latitude refers to imaginary lines that run east
and west around the planet, north and south of
Earth's equator. Areas near the equator receive
direct rays from the sun all year and have warm
temperatures. Higher latitudes receive fewer
direct rays and are cooler.

> **Why are areas near the equator warmer than those in higher latitudes?**
> _____
> _____

THE SEASONS

Many locations on Earth have four seasons:
winter, spring, summer, and fall. These are based
on temperature and how long the days are.

The seasons change because of the tilt of
Earth's axis. In summer, the Northern
Hemisphere is tilted toward the sun. It receives
more solar energy than during the winter, when it
is tilted away from the sun.

Because Earth's axis is tilted, the hemispheres
have opposite seasons. Winter in the Northern
Hemisphere is summer in the Southern
Hemisphere. During the fall and spring, the poles
point neither toward nor away from the sun. In
spring, temperatures rise and days become longer
as summer approaches. In fall, the opposite
occurs.

> **What would the seasons be like in the Northern and Southern Hemispheres if Earth's axis weren't tilted?**
> _____
> _____

In some regions, the seasons are tied to rainfall
instead of temperature. One of these regions,
close to the equator, is the **tropics.** There, winds
bring heavy rains from June to October. The
weather turns dry in the tropics from November
to January.

> **Circle the name of the warm region near the equator.**

CHALLENGE ACTIVITY

Critical Thinking: Draw Conclusions Imagine that
you are a travel agent. One of your clients is
planning a trip to Argentina in June, and another
is planning a trip to Chicago in August. What
kinds of clothing would you suggest they pack
for their trips and why?

| latitude | rainfall | revolution |
| rotation | solar energy | tropics |

DIRECTIONS On the line provided before each statement, write **T** if a statement is true and **F** if a statement is false. If the statement is false, write the term from the word bank that would make the statement correct on the line after each sentence.

_____ 1. The hemisphere of Earth that is tilted away from the sun receives less direct <u>rainfall</u> than the other hemisphere receives.

_____

_____ 2. An umbrella might be more useful to a person in the <u>tropics</u> than a winter coat.

_____

_____ 3. Earth's path, or orbit, around the sun is its <u>rotation</u>.

_____

_____ 4. One <u>revolution</u> of Earth takes 24 hours.

_____

_____ 5. Plants in an area of high latitude receive less direct solar energy during the year than plants at a <u>lower latitude</u> because they are farther from the equator.

_____

The Physical World

MAIN IDEAS

1. Salt water and freshwater make up Earth's water supply.
2. In the water cycle, water circulates from Earth's surface to the atmosphere and back again.
3. Water plays an important role in people's lives.

Key Terms and Places

freshwater water without salt

glaciers large areas of slow-moving ice

surface water water that is stored in Earth's streams, rivers, and lakes

precipitation water that falls to Earth's surface as rain, snow, sleet, or hail

groundwater water found below Earth's surface

water vapor water that occurs in the air as an invisible gas

water cycle the circulation of water from Earth's surface to the atmosphere and back

Lesson Summary
EARTH'S WATER SUPPLY

Approximately two-thirds of Earth's surface is covered with water. There are two kinds of water: salt water and **freshwater.** About 97 percent of Earth's water is salt water. Most of it is in the oceans, seas, gulfs, bays, and straits. Some lakes, such as the Great Salt Lake in Utah, also contain salt water.

Salt water cannot be used for drinking. Only freshwater is safe to drink. Freshwater is found in lakes and rivers and stored underground. Much is frozen in the ice found in **glaciers,** as well as the Arctic and Antarctic regions.

One form of freshwater is **surface water.** This is stored in streams, lakes, and rivers. Streams form when **precipitation** falls to Earth as rain, snow, sleet, or hail. These streams then flow into larger

> Circle the places where we find salt water.

> Underline the places where we find freshwater.

Guided Reading Workbook

streams and rivers. Less than 1 percent of Earth's water supply comes from surface water.

Most freshwater is stored underground. **Groundwater** bubbles to the surface in springs or can be reached by digging deep holes, or wells.

THE WATER CYCLE

Water is the only substance on Earth that can take the form of a liquid, gas, or solid. In its solid form, water is snow and ice. Liquid water is rain or water found in lakes and rivers. **Water vapor** is an invisible form of water in the air.

Water is always moving. When water on Earth's surface heats up, it evaporates and turns into water vapor. It then rises from Earth into the atmosphere. When it cools down, it changes from water vapor to liquid. Droplets of water form clouds. When they get heavier, these droplets fall to Earth as precipitation. This process of evaporation and precipitation is called the **water cycle.**

Some precipitation is absorbed into the soil as groundwater. The rest flows into streams, rivers, and oceans.

WATER AND PEOPLE

Water is crucial for survival. It is a problem when people lack freshwater because of shortages. Shortages are caused by overuse and by drought, when there is little or no precipitation for a long time. Water shortages can lead to less food. Another problem is pollution. Chemicals and waste can pollute water, making it dangerous to use. Lack of water can lead to conflicts when countries fight over who controls water supplies.

Water can affect the physical environment. For example, sinkholes are formed when water dissolves the surface layer of the ground. Heavy rains can cause flooding that damages property and threatens lives.

> Underline the words that define water vapor.

> What are the two main processes of the water cycle?
> _____
> _____

> Circle two words that are causes of water shortages.

> How does water cause sinkholes?
> _____
> _____

Water has many benefits, too. It quenches our thirst and allows us to have food to eat. Flowing water is an important source of electric energy. Water also provides recreation, making our lives richer and more enjoyable.

Water is essential for life on Earth. Cities and even nations are now working together to manage freshwater supplies. For example, Central Florida Water Initiative works with businesses and many other groups to protect the water resources in that region.

How does the Central Florida Water Initiative help water supplies?
_____
_____
_____
_____
_____

CHALLENGE ACTIVITY

Critical Thinking: Solve Problems You are campaigning for public office. Write a speech describing three actions you plan to take to protect supplies of freshwater.

DIRECTIONS Read each sentence, and fill in the blank with the word in the word pair that best completes the sentence.

1. Some freshwater is locked in Earth's _____. (**water vapor/ glaciers**)

2. Less than 1 percent of Earth's water supply comes from _____ stored in streams, rivers, and lakes. (**surface water/ groundwater**)

3. Water can be a solid (ice), a liquid, or a gas called _____. (**precipitation/water vapor**)

4. The water brought to the surface from deep holes is _____. (**freshwater/groundwater**)

5. _____ is water that falls from clouds as rain, snow, sleet, or hail. (**Precipitation/Water cycle**)

6. Surface water is a form of _____. (**glacier/freshwater**)

| freshwater | glacier | groundwater | precipitation |
| surface water | water cycle | water vapor | |

DIRECTIONS Use the terms from the word bank to write a summary of what you learned in the lesson.

_____

_____

_____

_____

_____

_____

_____

The Physical World

MAIN IDEAS
1. Earth's surface is covered by many different landforms.
2. Forces below Earth's surface build up our landforms.
3. Forces on the planet's surface shape Earth's landforms.
4. Landforms influence people's lives and culture.

Key Terms and Places

landforms shapes on Earth's surface, such as hills or mountains

continents large landmasses

plate tectonics theory suggesting that Earth's surface is divided into more than 12 slow-moving plates, or pieces of Earth's crust

lava magma, or liquid rock, that reaches Earth's surface

earthquakes sudden, violent movements of Earth's crust

weathering process of breaking rock into smaller pieces

erosion movement of sediment from one location to another

alluvial deposition process by which rivers create floodplains and deltas when they flood and deposit sediment along the banks

Lesson Summary
LANDFORMS

Geographers study **landforms** such as mountains, valleys, plains, islands, and peninsulas. They study how landforms are made and how they affect human activity.

> **Give two examples of landforms.**
> _____
> _____
> _____

FORCES BELOW EARTH'S SURFACE

The planet is made up of three layers. Below the top layer, or crust, is a layer of liquid. Earth's center, the third layer, is a solid core. The planet has seven **continents,** large landmasses that are part of Earth's crust. Earth's crust is divided into 12 pieces, called plates. These plates move very slowly. Geographers have a theory called **plate tectonics,** which explains how plates' movements shape our landforms.

> **What are plates?**
> _____
> _____

Energy from deep inside the planet makes the plates move at different speeds and in different directions. As they move, they shift the continents. This is known as continental drift. Plates move in three ways: they collide, they separate, and they slide past each other.

The energy of colliding plates creates new landforms. When two ocean plates collide, they may form deep valleys on the ocean's floor. When ocean plates collide with continental plates, mountain ranges are formed. Mountains are also created when two continental plates collide.

When plates separate, usually on the ocean floor, they cause gaps in the planet's crust. Magma, or liquid rock, rises through the cracks as **lava.** As it cools, it forms underwater mountains or ridges. Sometimes these mountains rise above the surface of the water and form islands.

Plates can also slide past each other. When they grind past each other, they cause **earthquakes.** Earthquakes often happen along faults, or breaks in Earth's crust.

PROCESSES ON EARTH'S SURFACE

As landforms are created, other forces work to wear them away. **Weathering** breaks larger rocks into smaller rocks. Changes in temperature can cause cracks in rocks. Water then gets into the cracks, expands as it freezes, and breaks the rocks. Rocks eventually break down into smaller pieces called sediment.

Another force that wears down landforms is **erosion.** Erosion takes place when sediment is moved by water, ice, and wind. The most common cause of erosion is water. Rivers can flood their banks and deposit sediment, a process called **alluvial deposition.** This creates floodplains and river deltas.

Underline the sentence that lists the three different ways in which Earth's plates move.

Underline what happens when two ocean plates collide with one another.

What causes earthquakes?
_____
_____

Circle the three elements that cause erosion.

Guided Reading Workbook

LANDFORMS INFLUENCE LIFE

Landforms influence where people live. For example, people might want to farm in an area with good soil and water. Mineral deposits may create jobs in mining. People also change landforms in many ways. For example, engineers build tunnels through mountains to make roads. Farmers build terraces on steep hillsides.

CHALLENGE ACTIVITY

Critical Thinking: Draw Inferences Find out about a landform in your area that was changed by people. Write a report explaining why and how it was changed.

DIRECTIONS Look at each set of four vocabulary terms. On the line provided, write the letter of the term that does not relate to the others.

_____ 1. a. erosion   b. weathering   c. landform   d. continent

_____ 2. a. lava   b. alluvial depositions   c. earthquake   d. plate tectonics

alluvial depositions	continents	earthquake	erosion
landforms	lava	plate tectonics	weathering

DIRECTIONS Answer each question by writing a sentence that contains at least one word from the word bank.

3. What are two ways that the movements of tectonic plates affect Earth?

_____

_____

4. What is the most common cause of erosion?

_____

_____

DIRECTIONS Choose four of the terms from the word bank. Look them up in a dictionary. Write the definition of the word that is closest to the definition that is used in your textbook.

_____

_____

_____

_____

The Physical World

MAIN IDEAS

1. While weather is short term, climate is a region's average weather over a long period.
2. The amount of sun at a given location is affected by Earth's tilt, movement, and shape.
3. Wind and water move heat around Earth, affecting how warm or wet a place is.
4. Mountains influence temperature and precipitation.

Key Terms and Places

weather short-term changes in the air for a given place and time

climate region's average weather conditions over a long period

prevailing winds winds that blow in the same direction over large areas of Earth

ocean currents large streams of surface seawater

front place where two air masses of different temperature or moisture content meet

Lesson Summary

UNDERSTANDING WEATHER AND CLIMATE

Weather is the temperature and precipitation at a specific time and place. **Climate** is a region's average weather over a long period of time. Climate and weather are affected by the sun, location on Earth, wind, water, and mountains.

> Circle the forces that affect climate and weather.

SUN AND LOCATION

The parts of Earth tilted toward the sun get more solar energy than the parts tilted away from the sun. This changes during the year, creating seasons. While some locations are having a warm summer, others are having a cold winter.

Energy from the sun falls more directly on the equator, so that area has warm temperatures all year. It gets colder as you move away from the low latitude of the equator. The coldest areas are at the poles, the highest latitudes.

> Underline the sentence that explains why the equator has warm temperatures year-round.

Guided Reading Workbook

Lesson 4, *continued*

WIND AND WATER

Heat from the sun moves around Earth, partly because of winds. Winds blow in great streams around the planet. They are caused by the rising and sinking of air. Cold air sinks and warm air rises. More air flows in to take the place of the air that has moved.

Prevailing winds are winds that blow in the same direction over large areas of Earth. Hot air rises at the equator and flows toward the poles. Cold air at the poles sinks and moves toward the equator. The planet's rotation curves the winds east or west. Prevailing winds control an area's climate. They make regions warmer or colder, drier or wetter. They pick up moisture from water and dry out as they pass over land.

Large bodies of water also affect temperature. **Ocean currents** are large streams of surface water that carry warm water from the equator toward the poles and cold water from the poles toward the equator. Water heats and cools more slowly than land. Therefore, water helps to moderate the temperature of nearby land, keeping it from getting very hot or very cold.

Storms happen when two large bodies of air collide. A **front** is a place where two air masses with different temperatures or moisture collide. In the United States and other regions, warm and cold air masses meet often, causing severe weather. These can include thunderstorms, blizzards, and tornadoes. Tornadoes are twisting funnels of air that touch the ground. Hurricanes are large tropical storms that form over water. They bring strong winds and heavy rain. Tornadoes and hurricanes are both dangerous and destructive.

> **What causes wind?**
> _____
> _____

> **Which heats and cools more slowly—land or water?**
> _____

> **What often happens when warm and cold air masses meet?**
> _____
> _____
> _____

Lesson 4, *continued*

MOUNTAINS

Mountains also affect climate. The higher areas are colder than the lower elevations. Warm air blowing against a mountainside rises and cools. Clouds form, and precipitation falls on the side facing the wind. However, there is little moisture on the other side of the mountain. This effect creates a rain shadow, a dry area on the side of the mountain facing away from the direction of the wind.

> **Which areas are colder— lower or higher elevations?**
> _____

CHALLENGE ACTIVITY

Critical Thinking: Sequence Write a short description of the process leading up to the formation of a rain shadow. Draw and label a picture to go with your description.

Guided Reading Workbook

DIRECTIONS On the line provided before each statement, write **T** if
a statement is true and **F** if a statement is false. If the statement is
false, write the correct term on the line after each sentence that
makes the sentence true.

_____ 1. <u>Climate</u> describes the atmospheric conditions in a place at a specific
time. It changes rapidly.

_____

_____

_____ 2. <u>Precipitation</u> falls on the side of a mountain that faces the wind.

_____

_____ 3. <u>Fronts</u> may form when air masses of different temperatures come
together.

_____

_____ 4. <u>Ocean currents</u> affect the temperature of nearby land.

_____

_____ 5. Warm air at the <u>poles</u> rises, causing prevailing winds that travel toward
the <u>equator</u>.

_____

_____

climate	equator	front	ocean currents
poles	precipitation	prevailing winds	weather

DIRECTIONS Choose five of the vocabulary words from the word
bank. On a separate sheet of paper, use these words to write a
summary of what you learned in the lesson.

_____

_____

_____

_____

_____

The Physical World

MAIN IDEAS

1. Geographers use temperature, precipitation, and plant life to identify climate zones.
2. Tropical climates are wet and warm, while dry climates receive little or no rain.
3. Temperate climates have the most seasonal change.
4. Polar climates are cold and dry, while highland climates change with elevation.

Key Terms and Places

monsoons winds that shift direction with the seasons and create wet and dry periods

savannas areas of tall grasses and scattered trees and shrubs

steppes semidry grasslands or prairies

permafrost permanently frozen layers of soil

Lesson Summary

MAJOR CLIMATE ZONES

We can divide Earth into five climate zones: tropical, temperate, polar, dry, and highland. Tropical climates appear near the equator, temperate climates are found in the middle latitudes, and polar climates occur near the poles. Dry and highland climates can appear at different latitudes.

> Underline the names of the five climate zones.

TROPICAL AND DRY CLIMATES

Humid tropical climates occur near the equator. Some are hot and humid throughout the year. Rain forests need this type of climate to thrive and support thousands of species. Other tropical areas have **monsoons**—winds that shift directions and create wet and dry seasons.

Moving away from the equator, we find tropical savanna climates. A long, hot dry season is followed by short periods of rain. This climate supports **savannas,** an area of tall grasses and scattered trees and shrubs.

> What happens when monsoon winds change direction?
>
> _____
>
> _____

Deserts are hot and dry. At night, the dry air cools quickly; desert nights can be cold. Only a few tough plants and animals survive in a desert. Sometimes **steppes**—semidry grasslands—are found near deserts.

TEMPERATE CLIMATES

Temperate, or mild, climates occur in the middle latitudes. In this climate, weather often changes quickly when cold and warm air masses meet. Most temperate regions have four distinct seasons, with hot summers and cold winters.

| Circle the name of the climate that can have four distinct seasons. |

A Mediterranean climate has hot, sunny summers and mild, wet winters. They occur near the ocean, and the climate is mostly pleasant. People like to vacation in these climates. Only small, scattered trees survive in these areas.

| What do people typically like to do in Mediterranean climates? _____ |

East coasts near the tropics have humid subtropical climates because winds bring moisture from the ocean. They have hot, wet summers and mild winters, with storms year-round. Marine west coast climates occur farther north on the west coast. They also get moisture from the sea, which causes mild summers and rainy winters. Inland or east-coast regions in the upper-middle latitudes often have humid continental climates. These have short, hot summers, a mild spring and fall, and long, cold winters.

| What kind of climate do you live in? _____ _____ _____ |

POLAR AND HIGHLAND CLIMATES

There are three polar climates. Subarctic climate occurs south of the Arctic Ocean. Winters are long and very cold; summers are cool. There is enough precipitation to support forests. At the same latitude near the coasts, tundra climate is also cold, but too dry for trees to survive. In parts of the tundra, soil is frozen as **permafrost.**

| Can there be forests in subarctic climates? Explain. _____ _____ _____ |

Ice cap climates are the coldest on Earth. There is little precipitation and little vegetation. Even though it is a harsh place, penguins and polar bears live there.

Highland, or mountain, climate changes with elevation. As you go up a mountain, the climate may go from tropical to polar.

CHALLENGE ACTIVITY

Critical Thinking: Compare and Contrast

Create a table showing the differences and similarities between any two types of climate.

DIRECTIONS Write three words or phrases that describe the term.

1. savanna _____

2. steppe _____

3. monsoon _____

_____

4. permafrost _____

_____

DIRECTIONS Look at each set of four terms. On the line provided, write the letter of the term that does not relate to the others.

_____ 5. a. humid continental
      b. marine west coast
      c. Mediterranean
      d. steppe

_____ 6. a. subarctic
      b. tundra
      c. desert
      d. permafrost

_____ 7. a. monsoon
      b. muggy
      c. prairies
      d. rain forest

_____ 8. a. forest
      b. steppes
      c. savannas
      d. grassland

The Physical World

> **MAIN IDEAS**
> 1. The environment and life are interconnected and exist in a fragile balance.
> 2. Soils play an important role in the environment.

Key Terms and Places

environment plant or animal's surroundings

ecosystem any place where plants and animals depend upon each other and their environment for survival

biome area much larger than an ecosystem and possibly made up of several ecosystems

habitat place where a plant or animal lives

extinct to die out completely

humus decayed plant or animal matter

desertification slow process of losing soil fertility and plant life

Lesson Summary
THE ENVIRONMENT AND LIFE

Plants and animals cannot live just anywhere. They must have an **environment,** or surroundings, that suits them. Climate, land features, and water are all part of a living thing's environment. Plants and animals adapt to specific environments. For example, kangaroo rats do not need to drink much water and are adapted to a desert environment.

An **ecosystem** is the connection between a particular environment and the plants and animals that live there. They all depend on each other for survival. Ecosystems can be as small as a garden pond or as large as a forest. **Biomes** are much larger than ecosystems. They may contain several ecosystems.

Each part of an ecosystem fills a certain role in a cycle. For example, the sun provides energy to plants, which use it to make food. These plants

> **Which is larger, a biome or an ecosystem?**
> _____

> **Underline the sentences that describe the steps in an ecosystem's cycle.**

Guided Reading Workbook

then provide energy and food to other plants and animals. When these life forms die, their bodies break down and give nutrients to the soil so more plants can grow.

A small change in one part of an ecosystem can affect the whole system. Many natural events and human actions affect ecosystems and the habitats in them. A **habitat** is the place where a plant or animal lives. Natural events include forest fires, disease, and climate changes.

> Circle the natural events that can affect ecosystems.

Human actions such as clearing land and polluting can destroy habitats. For example, people are clearing Earth's rain forests for farmland, lumber, and other reasons. As a result, these diverse habitats are being lost. If a change to the environment is extreme, a species might become **extinct,** or die out completely.

> What two human actions are destroying habitats?
> _____
> _____

Many countries are passing laws to protect the environment. Although these laws do not please everyone, they can have good results. The U.S. Endangered Species Act of 1973 has saved 47 species from becoming extinct.

SOIL AND THE ENVIRONMENT

An environment's soil affects which plants can grow there. Fertile soils have lots of humus and minerals. **Humus** is decayed plant or animal matter.

> Circle two things found in fertile soil.

Soils can lose fertility from erosion when wind or water sweeps topsoil away. Soil can also lose fertility from planting the same crops repeatedly. When soil becomes worn out and can no longer support plants, **desertification** can occur. The spread of desert conditions causes problems in many parts of the world.

CHALLENGE ACTIVITY

Critical Thinking: Draw Inferences Consider the interconnections in your environment. As you go through a normal day, keep a list of the sources you rely on for energy, food, and water.

DIRECTIONS Read each sentence and fill in the blank with the word in the word pair that best completes the sentence.

1. Organic material called _____ enriches the soil. (**biomes/humus**)

2. When soil gets worn out, it may lead to _____. (**erosion/desertification**)

3. A rainforest is a/an _____, which can contain many different ecosystems. (**biome/environment**)

4. If there are too many changes in conditions, a species may die out, or become _____. (**consequence/extinct**)

5. Plants and animals are adapted to the specific _____ where they live. (**environment/humus**)

6. Laws have been passed to protect _____ from human activities that could destroy them. (**habitats/nutrients**)

biome	desertification	ecosystem	environment
erosion	extinct	fertile soils	habitat
humus	nutrients		

DIRECTIONS Choose five of the words from the word bank. On a separate sheet of paper, use these words to write a poem or story that relates to the lesson.

The Physical World

MAIN IDEAS

1. Earth provides valuable resources for our use.
2. Energy resources provide fuel, heat, and electricity.
3. Mineral resources include metals, rocks, and salt.
4. Resources shape people's lives and countries' wealth.

Key Terms and Places

natural resource any material in nature that people use and value

renewable resources resources that can be replaced naturally

nonrenewable resources resources that cannot be replaced

deforestation loss of forestland

reforestation planting trees to replace lost forestland

fossil fuels nonrenewable resources formed from the remains of ancient plants and animals

hydroelectric power production of electricity by moving water

Lesson Summary
EARTH'S VALUABLE RESOURCES

Anything in nature that people use and value is a **natural resource.** Earth's most important natural resources are air, water, soils, forests, and minerals. We often use these resources to make something new. For example, we make paper from trees. Resources such as trees are called **renewable resources** because another tree can grow in its place. Resources that cannot be replaced, such as oil, are called **nonrenewable resources.**

Even though forests are renewable, we can cut down trees faster than they can grow. For example, in Brazil, illegal logging is destroying rain forests. The loss of forests is called **deforestation.** When we plant trees to replace lost forests, we call it **reforestation.**

Circle the natural resources that are most important.

Underline the sentence that explains why there is deforestation even though trees are renewable resources.

Guided Reading Workbook

ENERGY RESOURCES

Most of our energy comes from **fossil fuels,** which are formed from the remains of ancient living things. These include coal, oil, and natural gas.

We use coal mostly for electricity, but it causes air pollution. Since there is a lot of coal, people are trying to find cleaner ways to use it. Another fossil fuel is petroleum, or oil. It is used to make different kinds of fuels and heating oil. Oil can also be turned into plastics, cosmetics, and other products.

> Circle four products made from oil.

We depend on fossil fuels for much of our energy, so they are very valuable. However, fuel from oil can cause air and land pollution. Oil spills pollute the water and hurt wildlife. The cleanest fossil fuel is natural gas, which is used mainly for cooking and heating.

> What is the cleanest-burning fossil fuel?
> _____

Many scientists believe that burning fossil fuels causes climate change. They believe Earth's temperature is rising. More than 190 countries have signed the Kyoto Protocol, an agreement adopted in 1997 that sets targets to reduce emissions from burning fossil fuels. They hope this will reduce pollution from fossil fuels.

Renewable energy resources include **hydroelectric power**—the creation of electricity from the motion and movement of running water. This is accomplished mainly by building dams on rivers. Other renewable energy sources are wind and solar energy. Wind produces electricity with windmills, and solar energy uses the power of sunlight to generate electricity.

> Underline the sentence that explains why some people do not want to use nuclear energy.

One nonrenewable resource is nuclear energy. This type of energy is created by splitting atoms, small particles of matter. Although nuclear energy does not pollute the air, it does produce dangerous waste material that must be stored for thousands of years.

Guided Reading Workbook

MINERAL RESOURCES

Like oil, minerals are nonrenewable and can be very valuable. Minerals include metals, salt, rocks, and gemstones. Minerals like iron are used to make steel. We make buildings from stone and window glass from quartz. We also use minerals to make jewelry, coins, and many other common objects. Recycling minerals like aluminum in cans can make these resources last longer.

> **List four uses of minerals.**
> _____
> _____
> _____

RESOURCES AND PEOPLE

Natural resources vary from place to place. Some places are rich in natural resources. Resources such as fertile farmland, forests, and oil have helped the United States become a powerful country with a strong economy. Places with fewer resources do not have the wealth and choices of Americans.

Some countries use their resources to trade for resources they do not have. For example, many Middle Eastern countries are rich in oil but do not have water to grow food. They must use their oil profits to import food. Some of these countries are part of The Organization of the Petroleum Exporting Countries (OPEC). This group of 13 countries helps control oil prices so oil-producing countries can use the wealth to buy products they need.

> **What is OPEC?**
> _____
> _____
> _____

CHALLENGE ACTIVITY

Critical Thinking: Draw Inferences Write a short essay explaining how America's natural resources have helped it become a powerful country.

deforestation	electricity	fossil fuels
hydroelectric power	natural resources	nonrenewable resources
petroleum	reforestation	renewable resources

DIRECTIONS Answer each question by writing a sentence that contains at least one word from the word bank.

1. What problem is caused when trees are cut down faster than they can grow back? How can this problem be fixed?

_____

_____

_____

2. What are some examples of energy resources we can use instead of fossil fuels? List two types, and explain how they work.

_____

_____

_____

3. What may happen to a country that has only a few natural resources?

_____

_____

_____

DIRECTIONS Write three examples of each term.

4. natural resources _____

5. renewable resources _____

6. fossil fuels _____

The Human World

> **MAIN IDEAS**
> 1. Culture is the set of beliefs, goals, and practices that a group of people share.
> 2. The world includes many different culture groups.
> 3. New ideas and events lead to changes in culture.
> 4. The features common to all cultures are called cultural universals.
> 5. All societies have social institutions that help their groups survive.
> 6. Every culture expresses itself creatively in a variety of ways.
> 7. All societies use technology to help shape and control the environment.

Key Terms and Places

culture set of beliefs, values, and practices a group of people have in common

culture trait activity or behavior in which people often take part

culture region area in which people have many shared culture traits

ethnic group group of people who share a common culture and ancestry

multicultural society society that includes a variety of cultures in the same area

cultural diffusion spread of culture traits from one region to another

cultural universals features societies have developed that are common to all cultures

social institutions organized patterns of belief and behavior that focus on meeting societal needs

heritage wealth of cultural elements that has been passed down over generations

universal theme message about life or human nature that is meaningful across time and in all places

technology use of knowledge, tools, and skills to solve problems

Lesson Summary
WHAT IS CULTURE?

Culture is the set of beliefs, values, and practices a group of people have in common. Everything in day-to-day life is part of culture, including language, religion, clothes, music, and foods.

> Underline the sentence that lists some examples of culture.

People everywhere share certain basic cultural features, such as forming a government, educating children, and creating art or music. However, people practice these things in different ways, making each culture unique.

Culture traits are activities or behaviors in which people often take part, such as language and popular sports. People share some culture traits but not others. For example, people eat using forks, chopsticks, or their fingers in different areas.

Cultures are often passed from one generation to the next. They may be based on family traditions, like holiday customs, or laws and moral codes passed down within a society. Other factors that influence how cultures develop include immigrants moving to a new country, historical events, and the environment where people live and work.

> **What are three factors that influence how a culture develops?**
>
> _____
> _____
> _____
> _____
> _____

CULTURE GROUPS

There are thousands of different cultures in the world. People who share a culture are part of a culture group that may be based on things like age or religion.

A **culture region** is an area in which people have many shared culture traits such as language, religion, or lifestyle. A cultural region can extend over many countries. For example, most people in North Africa and Southeast Asia share the Arabic language and Muslim religion. Some countries, like Japan, may be a single culture region. Other countries may have several different culture regions.

> **Circle the country that is also a single cultural region.**

Often, cultural regions within a country are based on ethnic groups. An **ethnic group** is a group of people who often share cultural traits like language, foods, or religion. Sometimes, though, people who have the same religion are still in different ethnic groups, and different ethnic groups can have different religious beliefs.

Countries or areas with many ethnic groups are **multicultural societies**. Multiculturalism can create an interesting mix of ideas and practices, but it can also lead to conflict. In Canada, French Canadians want to separate from the rest of Canada. In Rwanda, a 1990s ethnic conflict led to extreme violence. In some countries, like the U.S., different ethnic groups cooperate and live side by side. That is because so many people have migrated to the country from all over the world and they celebrate their ethnic heritage.

> **Why are different ethnic groups likely to cooperate in the U.S.?**
> _____
> _____
> _____
> _____
> _____

CHANGES IN CULTURE

Cultures change constantly, sometimes quickly and sometimes over years. Two main causes of change are new ideas or contact with other societies. New technology like motion pictures and the Internet have changed how people spend their time and how they communicate. Contact with another culture may cause both to change. For example, both Spanish and Native American cultures changed when the Spanish arrived in the Americas.

> **Underline two sentences that describe examples that cause cultures to change.**

Cultural diffusion is the spread of culture traits from one part of the world to another. It occurs when people bring their culture to another country. This happens when people immigrate or when people trade goods in different regions. People also move to other countries to escape conflicts and wars.

> **What are three ways cultural diffusion occurs?**
> _____
> _____
> _____
> _____

WHAT DO ALL CULTURES HAVE IN COMMON?

All people have the same basic needs, such as food, clothing, and shelter. Geographers believe that all societies have developed **cultural universals**—specific features that meet basic needs. Three important cultural universals are social institutions, creative expressions, and technology.

BASIC SOCIAL INSTITUTIONS

Social institutions are organized patterns of belief and behavior that focus on meeting the needs of the society's members. The most basic social institutions are family, education, religion, government, and economy. These institutions are shaped by a group's cultural values and principles, which vary from culture to culture.

Family is the most basic social institution. The family cares for the children and provides support. They also teach the culture's values and traditions, often through elders. Family members may live together under one roof or be part of a whole village. Societies also pass on values and knowledge through education. For example, U.S. schools teach students how to be good citizens.

Although there are many religions, they all help explain the meanings of life and death and the difference between good and bad behavior. Religions' practices and traditions make them the source of many cultures' beliefs and attitudes. In all world regions, religion has inspired great works of devotion, including art and architecture.

Government is a system of leaders and laws that help people live together in their community or country. It defines standards, protects property and people's rights, and helps settle conflicts. A society's economy is its system of using resources to meet needs. Economic principles guide the way a nation does business.

CREATIVE EXPRESSIONS

Societies, like individuals, express themselves creatively. There are three main types of creative expression. Performing arts include music, theater, and dance. Visual arts include painting, sculpture, and architecture. Literary arts are related in words and language such as literature and folklore.

> **Circle the most basic social institutions.**

> **What do all religions have in common?**
> _____
> _____
> _____
> _____
> _____
> _____
> _____
> _____
> _____

> **What are the three main types of creative expressions?**
> _____
> _____

Creative expressions reflect a specific **heritage,** or wealth of cultural elements that have been passed down through generations. Creative expressions also express individual choices, as well as universal themes. A **universal theme** is a message about life that is true throughout time and in all places. This is true of art masterpieces that continue to speak to people everywhere.

SCIENCE AND TECHNOLOGY

Technology is the use of knowledge, tools, and skills to solve problems. Science is a way of understanding the world through observation and the testing of ideas. Technology is often developed to solve problems posed by the environment we live in. Its use is influenced by factors such as politics, economics, and belief systems. For example, some countries restrict Internet use. Advances in science and technology have made life easier and have changed society. Vaccines have prevented diseases. Electricity and computers have transformed daily life and work for most of the world's people.

What are three examples of technology that have changed lives?
_____
_____
_____

CHALLENGE ACTIVITY

Critical Thinking: Make Inferences Consider all of the parts of your culture that have been influenced by other cultures. During a normal day, keep a list of all the things you use or do that you think have been influenced by other cultures.

DIRECTIONS On the line provided before each statement, write **T** if
a statement is true and **F** if a statement is false. If the statement is
false, write the term that would make the statement correct on the
line after each sentence.

_T_ 1. The language you speak and the sports you play are examples of
<u>culture traits</u>.

_____

_F_ 2. <u>Cultural universals</u> can create an interesting mix of ideas but
sometimes can lead to conflict.

All people have the same basic needs like food, clothing.

_F_ 3. When more than one cultural group lives in an area, this is called a
<u>cultural diffusion</u>.

_____

_____ 4. A great masterpiece of art, music, or literature has a <u>universal theme</u>.

_____

_____ 5. Family, education, religion, and government are all examples of basic
<u>ethnic groups</u>.

_____

_____ 6. A <u>culture region</u> can be one country or many countries.

_____

cultural diffusion	culture region	culture trait	cultural universal
ethnic group	multicultural society	social institutions	universal theme

DIRECTIONS On a separate sheet of paper, use four of the terms
from the word bank to write a summary of what you learned in the
lesson.

The Human World

MAIN IDEAS
1. The study of population patterns helps geographers learn about the world.
2. Population statistics and trends are important measures of population change.

Key Terms and Places

population total number of people in a given area

population density measure of the number of people living in an area, usually expressed as persons per square mile or square kilometer

birthrate annual number of births per 1,000 people

migration process of moving from one place to live in another

Lesson Summary
POPULATION PATTERNS

Population is the total number of people in a given area. Population patterns show how human populations change over time and tell us much about our world.

Population density is a measure of the number of people living in an area, expressed as persons per square mile or square kilometer. The more people per square mile, the more crowded it is and more limited space is. In places with a high density, land is expensive, buildings are taller, and roads are more crowded. However, there are usually more resources and jobs. Places with low density have more space, less traffic, and more open land, but goods and services may be in short supply.

Areas that are less populated are usually difficult to live in. They may be deserts or mountains or have harsh climates that make survival harder. Large clusters of people tend to live in places with good agricultural climates, plenty of vegetation, minerals, and reliable water sources.

> Underline the two sentences that describe the effects of high population density on a place.

> What are conditions like in areas of low population density?
>
> _____
>
> _____

Lesson 2, *continued*

Often, desirable areas attract so many people that there is too much demand for resources. This can change the environment. For example, as regions make room for more people, the amount of available farmland shrinks and local ecosystems are in danger. There is more demand for food and water, which can lead to shortages.

What are three problems caused by population growth?
_____
_____
_____

POPULATION CHANGE

The number of people living in an area affects jobs, housing, schools, medical care, available food, and many other things. Geographers track population changes by studying important statistics, movement of people, and population trends.

Three statistics are important to studying a country's population over time. **Birthrate** is the annual number of births per 1,000 people. Death rate is the annual number of deaths per 1,000 people. The rate of natural increase is the rate at which a population is changing. It is determined by subtracting the death rate from the birthrate.

Underline the sentence that tells how to calculate the rate of natural increase.

A population is shrinking if the death rate is higher than the birthrate. In most countries, the birthrate is higher than the death rate, and those populations are growing. The United States has a low rate of natural increase and is growing slowly. Other countries, like Mali, have a high natural increase that could double its population in 20 years.

High rates can make it hard for countries to develop economically because they need to provide jobs, education, and medical care for a growing population. Many governments track population patterns so they can better address the needs of their citizens.

Migration is a common cause of population change. It is the process of moving from one place to live in another. People may be pushed to leave a place because of problems there, such as war,

Why do high rates of natural increase make it hard for a country to develop economically?
_____
_____
_____
_____

famine, drought, or lack of jobs. Other people may be pulled to move to find political or religious freedom or economic opportunities in a new place.

For thousands of years, Earth's population growth was slow and steady. In the last 200 years, it has grown very rapidly due to better health care and improved food production. Currently, many industrialized countries have low rates of natural increase, while countries that are less industrialized often have very high growth. Fast growth can put a strain on resources, jobs, and government aid.

> **Why has the world's population grown faster in the last 200 years?**
>
> _____
> _____
> _____

CHALLENGE ACTIVITY

Critical Thinking: Identify Cause and Effect Find out the population density of your city or town. Write down ways that this density affects your life and the lives of others.

Lesson 2, *continued*

DIRECTIONS Read each sentence, and fill in the blank with the word in the word pair that best completes the sentence.

1. The study of human _____ focuses on the total number of people in a given area. (**population/migration**)

2. Studying the _____ is one way to track the percentage of natural increase in the population. (**population density/birthrate**)

3. Calculating _____ can tell us whether a population is growing or shrinking. (**natural increase/population density**)

4. _____ is a common cause of population change. (**Birthrate/Migration**)

5. Land is more expensive in areas with higher _____. (**population density/population patterns**)

birthrate	migration	natural increase
population	population density	population patterns

DIRECTIONS Look up three terms from the word bank in a dictionary. On a separate sheet of paper, write the dictionary definition of the term that is closest to the definition used in your textbook. Then write a sentence using each term correctly.

Guided Reading Workbook

The Human World

MAIN IDEAS

1. Natural resources and trade routes are important factors in determining location for settlements.
2. Areas can be defined as urban or rural.
3. Spatial patterns describe ways that people build settlements.
4. New technology has improved the interaction of regions with nearby and distant places.

Key Terms and Places

settlement any place where a community is established

trade route path used by people for buying and selling goods

urban related to cities and their surrounding areas

suburb residential community immediately outside of a city

metropolitan area large urban area

megalopolis area where several metropolitan areas grow together

rural related to areas that are found outside of cities

spatial pattern placement of people and objects on Earth and the space between them

linear settlements communities grouped along the length of a resource

cluster settlements communities grouped around or at the center of a resource

grid settlements communities that are laid out according to a network of transportation routes

commerce substantial exchange of goods between cities, states, or countries

Lesson Summary
THE IMPORTANCE OF LOCATION

A **settlement** is any place where a community is started. Settlements can be as small as a remote island village or as large as a very populated city. People often settle near natural resources. Early settlements were near freshwater and good farmland. In the 1800s many cities started as mining centers near coal and iron resources.

Where do people often settle?

_____

_____

Trade routes are also important to settlements. A **trade route** is a path people use to sell and buy goods. Many settlements started on trade routes, and they grew into important trading centers where major routes met. These centers also were important politically because of their wealth and the different groups that met there.

> What two factors made some trading centers more important than others?
>
> _____
> _____
> _____
> _____

URBAN AND RURAL

Geographers classify settlements by certain patterns. **Urban** areas are cities and their surroundings. They are heavily populated and developed, with many buildings and roads. Most urban jobs are not related to the land. Small urban areas might include a city center and a **suburb,** which is a residential area just outside the city. A large urban area, called a **metropolitan area,** might include an entire city, a number of suburbs, and surrounding areas. When several metropolitan areas grow into each other, they form a **megalopolis.** An example of this is the cluster of cities that includes Boston, New York, Philadelphia, Baltimore, and Washington, DC.

> How is population density different in rural and urban areas?
>
> _____
> _____
> _____
> _____

Rural areas are found outside of cities. They are usually lightly populated and their economies are tied to the land. Many are built around agriculture, forestry, mining, and recreation.

SPATIAL PATTERNS

Geographers use **spatial patterns** to classify different ways settlements form. They describe how people and objects on Earth are placed in relation to each other. **Linear settlements** are grouped along the length of resource, such as a river. They usually form long, narrow patterns. **Cluster settlements** are grouped around a resource or at its center. For example, many communities are grouped around coal mining operations. **Grid settlements** are laid out along a network of transportation routes. They are

usually in urban areas and may follow a grid
made of roads, water routes, or train routes.

> **What type of area is most likely to have a grid settlement?**
> _____

REGIONS INTERACT

Commerce is the significant exchange of goods
between cities, states, or countries. Urban areas
are usually centers of commerce and trade, as
well as government. They are often hubs for
education, communication, transportation, and
innovation. That is why many people live in or
near urban areas.

Advances in television, satellites, computers,
and the Internet improved communication. This
made it easier for cities to create services aimed at
nearby regions. It helped them reach markets
around the world. Advances in transportation
have made the world seem smaller because it is
easier to travel great distances in a shorter
amount of time.

> **Circle two important advancements that have helped commerce in cities grow.**

CHALLENGE ACTIVITY

Critical Thinking: Identify Cause and Effect

Look into the history of the place where you live
and answer the following questions. What was the
main source of commerce when your area was
first settled? How did that affect where the
settlement was first built and its spatial pattern?
How has the area changed over the years?

DIRECTIONS Read each sentence and fill in the blank with the word in the word pair that best completes the sentence.

1. A metropolitan area usually contains a(n) _____ area. (**megalopolis/urban**)

2. A rural community is likely to have started as a _____ near a river. (**linear settlement/suburb**)

cluster settlements	commerce	grid settlement	linear settlement
megalopolis	metropolitan area	rural	settlement
spatial pattern	suburb	trade route	urban

DIRECTIONS On the line provided before each statement, write **T** if the statement is true and **F** if the statement is false. If the statement is false, write the term from the word bank that would make the statement correct on the line after each sentence.

_____ 3. The substantial exchange of goods between cities, states, or countries is called <u>trade route</u>.

_____

_____ 4. Cluster settlements are an example of a <u>metropolitan area</u>.

_____

_____ 5. A <u>suburb</u> is usually part of an urban area.

_____

_____ 6. Economies of <u>rural</u> areas are often built around agriculture, forestry, mining, and recreation.

_____

_____ 7. A <u>grid settlement</u> is laid out according to a network of transportation routes.

_____

MAIN IDEAS
1. Geographers examine how environmental conditions shape people's lives.
2. Human activity changes specific places, regions, and the world as a whole.

Key Terms and Places

terraced farming form of farming on steps carved into steep hillsides to create flat land for growing crops

slash-and-burn agriculture form of farming where trees and plants in heavily forested areas are cut down and burned to clear the land for growing crops

center-pivot irrigation system where a center sprinkler waters crops in a circular field

fracking process that uses large amounts of water and chemicals to break up rocks in order to extract gas or oil

Lesson Summary

RESPONDING TO THE ENVIRONMENT

Geographers are interested in how the environment shapes people's lives. They study human systems, like farming, to see how people respond to environmental conditions. Farming is an important example of the way humans respond to their environment. Over time, humans have developed practices that let them grow food in many types of environmental conditions.

Sometimes people have to change the land. For example, in Peru, ancient Inca carved steps into steep hillsides to create flat fields for crops. This is called **terraced farming.** In thickly forested areas, like the Amazon rain forest, some farmers use **slash-and-burn agriculture.** They cut down trees and then burn them so they can clear land to grow crops. And in the U.S., farmers in dry areas create circular fields so they can water them

What is an example of a human system?   _____

What is the practice of carving steps into hillsides called?   _____

with a central sprinkler system called **center-pivot irrigation.**

Sometimes the environment cannot be controlled by humans. Natural hazards like fires, tornados, earthquakes, and hurricanes can be deadly and cause a lot of damage. People prepare for them by building shelters, practicing emergency drills, and following strict building codes.

CHANGING THE ENVIRONMENT

People have always changed their environment by building roads, bridges, and dams. They clear land for farming and housing and dig to find natural resources that give them fuel. Many human activities improve people's lives, but they are not always good for the environment. A dam could destroy the ecosystem of a river. Large cities trap heat and make areas drier.

> Circle six examples of ways humans have changed their environment.

Geographers worry about how humans may create environmental problems like pollution, acid rain, land erosion, and global warming. One concern is the ozone layer, which protects Earth from the sun's harmful rays. The use of products with chemicals called chlorofluorocarbons (CFS) started thinning out the ozone layer. Even though most CFS use has been stopped, the ozone layer has not recovered. It may be one of the causes of global warming, severe storms, and rising sea levels.

> Underline the sentence that explains how the ozone layer helps the planet.

Another concern is **fracking.** This process breaks up rock by injecting large amounts of water and chemicals into cracks. Some people support this process because it supplies oil and natural gas for fuel. Others are against fracking because they are worried it will hurt the environment or pollute drinking water.

> Why do some people support fracking?
>
> _____
>
> _____

Governments and environmental groups try to create laws to protect the environment and preserve natural resources. Other groups believe that some practices are important for economic growth. No matter what the viewpoint, environmental issues affect everyone on Earth. That is why many countries are now coming together to improve the environment around the globe.

CHALLENGE ACTIVITY

Critical Thinking: Draw Conclusions Write a paragraph that explains why some people are for fracking and some are against it. Use these arguments to come up with your own conclusion about whether to support or oppose fracking.

DIRECTIONS Write three words or phrases to describe each term.

1. slash-and-burn agriculture _____

   _____

2. terraced farming _____

   _____

3. center-pivot irrigation _____

4. fracking _____

   _____

| center-pivot irrigation | environment | fracking |
| ozone layer | slash-and-burn agriculture | terraced farming |

DIRECTIONS On a separate sheet of paper, use at least three terms from the word bank to write a short story about what you learned in the lesson.

Guided Reading Workbook

Government and Citizenship

MAIN IDEAS
1. The world is divided into physical and human borders.
2. The nations of the world interact through trade and foreign policy.
3. The nations of the world form a world community that resolves conflicts and addresses global issues.

Key Terms and Places

borders a country's political boundaries

sovereign nation government having complete authority over a geographic area

foreign policy a nation's plan for interacting with other countries of the world

diplomacy process of conducting relations between countries

national interest a country's economic, cultural, or military goals

United Nations an organization of the world's countries that promotes peace and security around the globe

human rights rights that all people deserve, such as rights to equality and justice

humanitarian aid assistance to people in distress

Lesson Summary
BOUNDARIES AND BORDERS

Every country has political boundaries, or **borders,** which mark its territory. Within a country, smaller political units such as cities, counties, and states each have their own borders. There are two main types of political boundaries: physical borders and human borders. Physical features such as mountains, deserts, lakes, and oceans make physical borders. These physical features rarely shift. Rivers are also used as boundaries, but the changing course of a river can create border difficulties.

There are two main types of human borders: cultural and geometric. A cultural boundary based on religion was used to divide Muslim Pakistan from mostly Hindu India. Geometric boundaries are borders that do not follow

> **What are the two main types of political boundaries?**
>
> _____
>
> _____

national or cultural patterns. Often, they are straight lines based on lines of latitude or longitude.

NATIONS OF THE WORLD

The establishment of borders is one of the characteristics of a **sovereign nation,** or a government that has complete authority over a geographic area. Sovereign nations rule independently from governments outside their borders. They rule over everyone in their territory and make decisions about domestic, or internal, affairs. They can also defend themselves against foreign invasion.

> Underline the sentence describing a sovereign nation's authority within its borders.

Sovereign nations interact with other nations through trade and **foreign policy.** Trade allows nations to get the goods they need in exchange for the goods they have or can make. A nation's foreign policy is its plan for interacting with other countries of the world. Foreign policy tools include **diplomacy** and foreign aid. Diplomacy is the process of conducting relations between countries. Diplomacy is used to maintain national security, prevent war, negotiate an end to conflicts, solve problems, and establish communication between countries. Foreign aid is economic or military assistance to another country. Each country shapes its foreign policy to help reach its economic, cultural, or military goals. These make up its **national interest.**

> List two foreign policy tools.
> _____

A WORLD COMMUNITY

Nations around the world are connected closely through trade, diplomacy, and foreign aid. What happens in one place affects others. The world community works together to promote cooperation between countries. When conflicts occur, countries from around the world try to settle them. The **United Nations** (UN) is an

Guided Reading Workbook

Lesson 1, *continued*

association of nearly 200 countries dedicated to promoting peace and security. It also works to guarantee **human rights,** or rights that all people deserve. These rights include political rights, social and economic rights, freedom of expression, and equality before the law. The UN sometimes places sanctions, or penalties, on countries, groups, or individuals who have broken international laws.

> **Underline the sentence that describes the main goals of the United Nations.**

Some groups provide humanitarian and development assistance to conflict- and poverty-stricken countries around the world. Humanitarian organizations providing aid in areas of conflict are protected by the Geneva Conventions. The Geneva Conventions are international humanitarian laws that regulate the conduct of armed conflict in all nations. They protect civilians, medics, and aid workers, along with the wounded, sick, and prisoners of war.

> **What are the Geneva Conventions?**
> _____
> _____
> _____
> _____
> _____
> _____
> _____

Crises such as earthquakes, floods, droughts, or tsunamis can leave people in great need. Groups from around the world provide **humanitarian aid,** or assistance to people in distress. Some groups aid refugees or provide medical care and vaccinations.

CHALLENGE ACTIVITY

Critical Thinking: Draw Conclusions

Look at a map showing the border between Canada and the United States. Write a description of the border using the following words: physical borders, human borders, and geometric borders.

DIRECTIONS Read each sentence, and fill in the blank with the word in the word pair that best completes the sentence.

1. There are two main types of ___borders___, physical and human. (**borders/humanitarian aid**)

2. A government that rules over everyone in its territory and makes decisions about domestic affairs is a ___sovereign___. (**sovereign nation/ United Nations**)

3. A nation's plan for interacting with other countries is its ___diplomacy___. (**diplomacy/foreign policy**)

4. A nation's economic, cultural, or military goals make up its ___national interest___. (**foreign policy/national interest**)

5. The process of conducting relations between countries is called ___Foreign___. (**diplomacy/foreign policy**)

6. Freedom of expression and equality before the law are examples of ___Human rights___. (**diplomacy/human rights**)

borders	diplomacy	foreign policy
human rights	humanitarian aid	national interest
sovereign nation	United Nations	

DIRECTIONS Answer each question by writing a sentence that contains at least two terms from the word bank.

7. What is the purpose of political boundaries?

___the purpose of political boundaries are___

8. How do sovereign nations interact with one another?

___sovereign nations interact with one another___

9. How do countries around the world deal with conflict and disaster?

___countries around the world deal with___
___conflict and disaster.___

66
62

Government and Citizenship

MAIN IDEAS
1. Limited governments of the world include democracies.
2. Unlimited governments of the world include totalitarian governments.
3. Most human rights abuses occur under unlimited governments of the world.

Key Terms and Places

limited government government that has legal limits on its power

constitution written plan of government that outlines its purposes, powers, and limitations

democracy form of government in which the people elect leaders and rule by majority

direct democracy government in which citizens meet in popular assembly to discuss issues and vote for leaders

representative democracy indirect democracy in which citizens vote for representatives who decide on issues and make laws on their behalf

common good welfare of the community

unlimited government government in which power is concentrated in the hands of a single leader or small group

totalitarian government government that controls all aspects of society

Lesson Summary
LIMITED GOVERNMENT

Governments make and enforce laws, regulate business and trade, and provide aid to people. A **limited government** has legal limits on its power, usually in the form of a constitution. A **constitution** is a written plan outlining the government's purposes, powers, and limitations. A **democracy** is a form of limited government in which the people elect leaders and rule by majority. In a **direct democracy,** citizens meet regularly in assembly to discuss issues and vote for leaders.

Most democratic governments today are **representative democracies.** The citizens vote for representatives to decide on issues and make laws

> **What is a constitution?**
> _____
> _____
> _____
> _____
> _____

on their behalf. Two major forms of representative democratic governments today are presidential and parliamentary democracies. In a presidential democracy, the president is elected by the people and is directly accountable to them. Power is shared among three branches of government. In a parliamentary democracy, the head of government is directly accountable to the legislature, or parliament. The legislative branch also holds executive functions. Most of the world's democratic governments today are parliamentary democracies. A few nations are also constitutional monarchies.

> Underline the two forms of representative democracies most common today.

In a limited government, both the government and individuals must obey the laws. These governments balance the welfare of the community, or the **common good,** with individual welfare. Democracies have social welfare systems that seek to improve the quality of their citizens' lives, and they protect their citizens' rights and freedoms.

> What two things do limited governments balance?
>
> _____
> _____
> _____
> _____

UNLIMITED GOVERNMENTS

In a limited government, everyone, including leaders, must obey the law. In an **unlimited government,** there are no limits on a ruler's power. Power in an authoritarian government is concentrated in the hands of a single leader or group. A **totalitarian government** is authoritarian rule at its most extreme. Totalitarian governments exercise control over all aspects of society—the government, economy, and even people's beliefs and actions. In these societies, citizens have no way to change the government. Examples of totalitarian governments include China under Mao Zedong and North Korea under Kim Jong-un.

> List two examples of totalitarian governments.
>
> _____
> _____

In unlimited governments, the rights of citizens are rarely recognized or protected, and citizens may not be able to take part in government or

Lesson 2, *continued*

openly express their views. Rulers often use force to put down opposition movements. They ignore or change constitutions or laws intended to restrict their power.

Shortly after World War II, the Chinese government created an authoritarian Communist system, imprisoning or killing those who spoke out against its policies. Although plans for industrial development were instituted, widespread food shortages led to the deaths of tens of millions by the early 1960s.

A gradual retreat from many of these early policies began in the late 1970s, but there were limits to what officials would allow. In 1989 the government violently crushed a peaceful pro-democracy student demonstration in China's capital, Beijing. This became known as the Tiananmen Square Massacre.

China's government today is balancing authoritarian rule, economic growth, and slow political reform.

What was the name given to the 1989 pro-democracy demonstration in Beijing?

_____

_____

HUMAN RIGHTS ABUSES

People today believe that everyone has human rights, or rights that all people deserve. These rights include equality, justice, political rights, and social and economic rights. Human rights abuses are most common in countries that are not free or are only partially free. These abuses include torture, slavery, and murder. Abuses in democratic countries often occur as a result of inaction.

The United Nations (UN) is an international organization committed to guaranteeing human rights for all people. The United States recognizes that respect for human rights promotes peace and deters aggression.

What are some examples of human rights abuses?

_____

_____

Guided Reading Workbook

CHALLENGE ACTIVITY

Critical Thinking: Compare and Contrast Write a
paragraph that compares and contrasts limited
and unlimited governments.

common good	constitution	democracy
direct democracy	unlimited government	representative democracy
totalitarian government		

DIRECTIONS On the line provided before each statement, write **T** if
a statement is true and **F** if a statement is false. If the statement is
false, write a term from the word bank that would make the
statement correct on the line after each sentence.

_____ 1. Korea under Kim Jong-un is an example of a <u>direct democracy</u>.

_____

_____ 2. <u>Democracy</u> is a form of government in which one person or a few
people hold power.

_____

_____ 3. A government in which the state has control over all aspects of society
is called a <u>totalitarian government</u>.

_____

_____ 4. In <u>unlimited governments,</u> people elect leaders and rule by majorities.

_____

_____ 5. A <u>constitution</u> enforces the legal limits of a government's power.

_____

_____ 6. A constitutional monarchy is an example of a <u>totalitarian government</u>.

_____

_____ 7. The welfare of a whole community is known as the <u>common good</u>.

_____

Government and Citizenship

MAIN IDEAS

1. The duties and roles of citizenship help to make representative government work.
2. Good citizens accept their responsibilities for maintaining a strong democracy.
3. Citizens influence government through public opinion.
4. The type of government in some societies influences the roles of the citizens in those societies.

Key Terms and Places

representative government system in which people are the ultimate source of government authority

draft law that requires men of certain ages and qualifications to join the military

jury duty required service of citizens to act as a member of a jury

political party group of citizens with similar views on public issues who work to put their ideas into effective government action

interest groups organizations of people with a common interest that try to influence government policies and decisions

public opinion the way large groups of citizens think about issues and people

nonrepresentative government a government in which government power is unlimited and citizens have few, if any, rights

Lesson Summary
DUTIES AND ROLES OF CITIZENSHIP

In the United States, citizens are the ultimate source of government authority. This is called a **representative government.** For this type of government to work, citizens must perform certain duties. One duty of citizens is to obey the law. A democracy needs educated citizens to choose leaders and understand issues. In the United States, you must attend school until the age of 16.

Who is the source of government authority in a representative government?

_____

Guided Reading Workbook

Citizens must pay taxes. Taxes fund public services such as road repair, police protection, and national security. When the country needs people to fight wars, it may issue a **draft.** A draft requires men of certain ages and qualifications to serve in the military. Citizens must also serve on a jury if they are called to do so. This service is called **jury duty.** The Constitution guarantees citizens the right to a trial by their peers—their fellow citizens.

| Underline the three responsibilities of citizens. |

RIGHTS AND RESPONSIBILITIES

In a representative government, citizens also have responsibilities—tasks they should do as citizens but that are not required by law.

In order to give consent to our lawmakers in government, we should vote. Voting is a way to show our decision makers whether we agree with their opinions on issues. Becoming informed about key issues, candidates, and current events will help you make informed choices when you vote. You might also take part in government by joining a **political party.** Political parties nominate or select candidates to run for political office.

Citizens can also join an **interest group.** These are organizations made up of people sharing a common goal. Interest groups try to influence government policies and decisions.

Another way to help society is by volunteering in your community. By knowing your own rights as a citizen, you can make sure you respect the rights of the people around you. You should also know if someone else's rights are being violated.

| What are some of our responsibilities as citizens?
_____
_____
_____
_____
_____
_____ |

CITIZENS AND THE MEDIA

The media plays an important role in free societies such as the United States. Newspapers, magazines, radio, television, film, the Internet, and books help to keep people informed. What citizens learn from the media shapes

| Underline the influences that affect public opinion. |

public opinion, or the way large groups of citizens think about issues and people. Public opinion on any particular issue may be very diverse.

Opinions are also influenced by family, friends, teachers, and clubs. Citizens rely on mass media to help them decide how to vote on important issues or candidates. However, effective citizenship requires critical thinking about what you see, hear, and read.

CITIZENSHIP IN OTHER SOCIETIES

Other representative governments may have similar roles and responsibilities for their citizens. These may not be the same as those of U.S. citizens. **Nonrepresentative governments** are governments in which citizens have few, if any, rights. The government maintains all the power. At times, citizens become so dissatisfied that they revolt against their leaders.

> What rights do citizens have under nonrepresentative governments?
> _____
> _____
> _____
> _____

CHALLENGE ACTIVITY

Critical Thinking: Explain Explain why representative government requires the involvement of the country's citizens.

draft	interest group	jury duty	nonrepresentative government
political party	public opinion	representative government	

DIRECTIONS Answer each question by writing a sentence that contains at least one term from the word bank.

1. How does a representative government work?

_____

_____

2. When might the United States issue a draft?

_____

_____

3. Name some duties and responsibilities of a United States citizen.

_____

_____

4. What is a nonrepresentative government?

_____

_____

5. Explain how the Constitution guarantees citizens a right to a trial by their peers.

_____

_____

6. How are candidates for political office usually chosen?

_____

_____

7. How can citizens in the United States influence the government?

_____

_____

Economics

MAIN IDEAS
1. The main problem in economics is scarcity.
2. Scarcity shapes how societies use factors of production.

Key Terms and Places

economy system of producing, selling, and buying goods and services

scarcity problem of having unlimited human wants in a world of limited resources

opportunity cost value of the thing given up when a choice is made

profit money an individual or business has left after paying expenses

factors of production basic economic resources needed to produce goods and services

contraction problem that can occur when a factor of production is in short supply

expansion benefit that can happen when a factor of production is increased

economic interdependence system in which one nation depends on another to provide goods and services it does not produce

Lesson Summary
KEY CONCEPTS

An **economy** is a system of producing, selling, and buying goods and services. There are global, national, and local economies. Goods are products that people buy and use such as clothes, furniture, and toothpaste. Services are actions that people provide such as styling hair, repairing cars, or mowing lawns. Consumers are the people who buy goods or services for personal use. The study of economies is called economics.

All economies face the same basic problem, called **scarcity.** People's wants are unlimited, but the resources available to satisfy their wants are limited. This leads to scarcity.

How are goods different from services?
_____
_____
_____
_____

Lesson 1, *continued*

Scarcity causes people to make choices, or tradeoffs, between things they need and things they want. Since every choice to buy something is a choice not to buy something else, every choice has an **opportunity cost.** This is the value of the thing given up in any choice or tradeoff. These choices by consumers help determine what sellers will produce and what they will charge for it. *Supply* is the amount of a good and service that businesses produce. *Demand* is the desire to have a good or service and the ability to pay for it. Supply and demand generally determine the price of a good or service. Businesses will produce more goods or services when they can charge a high price for it. Consumers prefer to buy more goods or services when the price is low. If the prices of goods or services rise, consumers will buy less.

What two factors generally determine the price of a good or service?
_____

Incentives, or benefits, influence economic choices. **Profit** is a major incentive for individuals and businesses. Profit is the money left after paying expenses. The desire to make money, or the profit incentive, leads many people to start a business. Consumer incentives include saving money and receiving something extra with a purchase.

Underline three economic incentives.

SCARCITY AND RESOURCE USE

There are three basic questions that must be answered when producing goods and services: What will be produced? How will it be produced? For whom will it be produced? Economists study **factors of production** to understand how societies answer these questions. There are four main factors of production: *natural resources, capital, labor,* and *entrepreneurs.* There is a limited supply of each factor. If a factor of production is in short supply, the situation could cause a **contraction** of the business. On the other hand, if

Circle the three basic questions for producing goods and services.

© Houghton Mifflin Harcourt Publishing Company

Guided Reading Workbook

Economics

MAIN IDEAS
1. There are three basic types of economic systems.
2. Contemporary societies have mixed economies.
3. The United States benefits from a free enterprise system.
4. Governments provide public goods.
5. Geographers categorize countries based on levels of economic development and range of economic activities.

Key Terms and Places

traditional economy people's work is based on long-established customs

command economy government controls the economy

market economy economy based on private ownership, free trade, and competition

mixed economy combination of traditional, market, and command economic systems

free enterprise system economic system in which few limits are placed on business activities

public goods goods and services provided by the government for public consumption

agricultural industries businesses that focus on growing crops and raising livestock

manufacturing industries businesses that make finished products from raw materials

wholesale industries businesses that sell to other businesses

retail industries businesses that sell directly to consumers

service industries businesses that provide services rather than goods

developed countries countries with strong economies and a high quality of life

developing countries countries with weak economies and a lower quality of life

gross domestic product (GDP) value of all goods and services produced within a country in a single year

Lesson Summary
MAIN TYPES OF ECONOMIC SYSTEMS

An economic system is the way in which a society organizes the production and distribution of goods and services. A **traditional economy** is based on long-established customs of who does what work. A **command economy** is controlled by

> Underline the three types of economic systems.

the government. A **market economy** is based on private ownership, free trade, and competition.

MODERN ECONOMIES

Most countries have one of three types of **mixed economies:** communist, capitalist, and socialist. In a communist society, the government owns all factors of production. In a capitalist economy, individuals and businesses own the factors of production. In socialist economies, the government controls some of the basic factors of production.

What are the three types of mixed economies?
_____
_____

THE FREE ENTERPRISE SYSTEM

U.S. capitalism is sometimes called the **free enterprise system.** Individuals are free to exchange goods and services and to own and operate businesses with little government intervention. The ability to make a profit is one of the key advantages of this system. To function properly, the free enterprise system requires that people obey laws, be truthful, and avoid behaviors that harm others.

What is a free enterprise system?
_____
_____
_____
_____
_____

GOVERNMENT AND PUBLIC GOODS

Governments today provide expensive or important services to large groups of people who might otherwise have to do without the service. These government goods and services are called **public goods.** They include schools, highways, and police and fire protection. Public goods are paid for through taxes. Because scarcity affects government, too, a government must determine the opportunity cost of public goods.

How are public goods paid?
_____

Governments also use regulations, or rules, to control business behavior. These rules must be helpful and fair. The most common government regulations include protection for public health and safety and for the environment.

Economics

MAIN IDEAS
1. Money is used as a medium of exchange, a store of value, and a unit of account.
2. Banks are places to store money, earn money, and borrow money.
3. People can use their earnings to build wealth.

Key Terms and Places

barter trade a good or service for a good or service provided by someone else

money anything that people will accept as payment for goods and services

medium of exchange means through which goods and services can be exchanged

store of value something that holds its value over time

unit of account yardstick of economic value in exchanges

interest rate percentage of the total amount of money loaned or borrowed

assets things of economic value that a person or company owns

income money paid to a person or business for goods or services

savings income not spent on immediate wants

investment use of money today in a way that earns future benefits

Lesson Summary
PURPOSES OF MONEY

Without money, people must **barter,** or trade, for goods and services they want or need. Barter works when both people want to exchange particular goods or services at the same time. If only one wants to exchange, barter does not work. This difficulty led to the invention of money. **Money** is anything that people will accept as payment for goods and services. Today it is generally metal coins or paper currency, but other items have been used as money.

Money performs three functions. First, it serves as a **medium of exchange,** or means through which goods and services can be exchanged. Second, it serves as a **store of value,** something that holds its value over time. This

> **Why is money easier to use than barter?**
> _____
> _____
> _____
> _____
> _____
> _____
> _____

> **Underline the three functions of money.**

Guided Reading Workbook

Lesson 3, *continued*

allows money to be saved for use in the future. Third, money serves as a **unit of account.** It allows people to measure the relative costs of goods and services. In the United States, the economic value of all goods and services can be measured by the dollar, the nation's basic monetary unit.

BANKS AND THE ECONOMY

Banks are like money stores, where people buy (borrow) money and sell (lend) it. Customers store money, earn money, and borrow money at a bank. Banks are businesses, so they earn money by charging interest or fees for these services.

> **How do banks earn money?**
> _____
> _____
> _____

Banks have three main functions. First, they are safe places where people can store money. Second, customers can earn money when they store their savings in banks. Savings accounts and some checking accounts offer a payment, called interest. The bank is borrowing the money from the customer, and the customer is paid for the use of the money. Third, banks loan this money to other customers who want to borrow money for a purchase. These borrowers pay the bank interest for the use of the money. The amount of interest paid is based on an **interest rate.** When interest rates are high, people are more likely to save their money. When interest rates are low, they may borrow or shift their savings to investments with higher interest rates.

> **Underline the three main functions of banks.**

MONEY MANAGEMENT

People and businesses save and invest money in order to increase their financial resources. Savings and investments are good ways to gain **assets,** which are things a person or business owns that have economic value.

Every person who has a job that pays a wage earns **income.** Businesses also earn income by

Guided Reading Workbook

Economics

> **MAIN IDEAS**
> 1. Globalization links the world's countries together through culture and trade.
> 2. Multinational corporations make global trade easier and allow countries to become more interdependent.
> 3. The world community works together to solve global conflicts and crises.

Key Terms and Places

globalization process in which countries are increasingly linked to each other through culture and trade

popular culture culture traits that are well known and widely accepted

trade barriers any law that limits free trade between nations

free trade trade without trade barriers between nations

Lesson Summary
GLOBALIZATION

People around the world are more closely linked than ever before. **Globalization** is the process in which countries are increasingly linked to each other through culture and trade. Improvements in transportation and communication have increased globalization.

> Underline the sentence that describes two ways countries are linked together.

   Popular culture refers to culture traits that are well known and widely accepted. These traits can include food, sports, music, and movies. The United States has a great influence on popular culture through American products, television, and the English language. English has become the major global language. It is used for international music, business, science, and education around the world. The United States is, in turn, greatly influenced by other countries. Martial arts movies from Asia are quite popular in the United States, and many foreign words such as *sushi* and *croissant* have become common in the English language.

> What are four traits that can be considered part of popular culture?
>
> _____
> _____
> _____
> _____

           Guided Reading Workbook

GLOBAL TRADE

Globalization also connects businesses and affects trade. Global trade takes place at a much faster pace than ever because of faster transportation and communication technologies. Telecommunication, computers, and the Internet have made global trade quick and easy.

The expansion of global trade has increased interdependence among the world's countries. Interdependence is a relationship between countries in which they rely on one another for resources, goods, or services. Companies that operate in a number of different countries are called multinational corporations. For their manufacturing plants, these companies select locations where raw materials or labor is cheapest. They often produce different parts of their products on different continents. Many developing nations want multinational corporations to invest in them because they create jobs.

What four improvements have made global trade faster and easier?
_____
_____
_____

Why do many developing nations want multinational corporations to invest in them?
_____
_____
_____

GLOBAL ECONOMIC ISSUES

Countries trade with each other to obtain resources, goods, and services. Developing nations still struggle to gain economic stability because they lack the necessary technologies, well-trained workers, and money for investments. Developed nations provide aid to developing nations through the work of international organizations. The World Bank provides loans for large projects, health care, education, or infrastructure such as roads or power plants. The International Monetary Fund (IMF) offers emergency loans to countries in financial trouble.

Sometimes, governments pass laws to protect their countries' jobs and industries. **Trade barriers** such as quotas, tariffs, and embargoes limit **free trade** between nations. Quotas limit the number of lower-priced products that can be imported. A tariff, or tax on imported goods, protects the

What are two international organizations that aid developing nations?
_____
_____

growing food is so important it is called the
Neolithic Revolution.

Farm settlements formed in Mesopotamia as
early as 7000 BC. Every year, floods on the rivers
brought **silt**. The fertile silt made the land ideal
for farming. Farmers grew wheat, barley, and
other grains. Livestock, birds, and fish were also
sources of food.

Plentiful food led to population growth and
villages formed. Eventually, these early villages
developed into the world's first **civilization**.
Civilizations usually have certain features, such
as large cities with different types of people.
They have culture like writing, education, art,
and architecture. Governments with leaders and
laws help civilizations develop. The governments
make economic decisions that can improve
people's lives.

FARMING AND CITIES

Early farmers faced the challenge of learning
how to control the flow of river water to their
fields in both rainy and dry seasons. Flooding
destroyed crops, killed livestock, and washed
away homes. When water levels were too low,
crops dried up.

To solve their problems, Mesopotamians used
irrigation. They dug out large storage basins to
catch rainwater. Then they dug **canals** that
connected these basins to a network of ditches.
These ditches brought water to the fields. To
protect the fields from flooding, farmers built up
riverbanks. This held back floodwaters even when
river levels were high.

Irrigation increased the amount of food
farmers could grow and gave them water to graze
cattle and sheep. This provided a variety of foods
and led to a food **surplus**. Fewer people needed to
farm, and they started doing other jobs.

> **Why is silt important?**
> _____
> _____
> _____

> **Circle four features of a civilization.**

> **Underline the sentence that lists some of the problems caused by flooding.**

> **How did Mesopotamians move water from storage basins to irrigation ditches?**
> _____

Guided Reading Workbook

For the first time, people became crafters, religious leaders, and government workers. A **division of labor** developed, where specialized workers could work on different parts of large projects. This helped society accomplish more, but it also required order. So Mesopotamians created structure and rules through laws and government.

Mesopotamian settlements grew in size and complexity between 4000 and 3000 BC. Most people continued to work in farming jobs. However, cities became important places. People traded goods in cities. Cities became the political, religious, cultural, and economic centers of Mesopotamian civilization.

> **Why were cities important to Mesopotamian civilization?**
>
> _____
>
> _____
>
> _____

CHALLENGE ACTIVITY

Critical Thinking: Draw Inferences Use information from this lesson to list six jobs Mesopotamians might have had.

Another society called the Akkadians developed along the Tigris and Euphrates rivers, north of Sumer. They lived in peace with the Sumerians until the 2300s BC. The Akkadian leader Sargon wanted to extend his territory. He built a large permanent army and defeated all the city-states of Sumer as well as all of northern Mesopotamia. With these conquests, Sargon established the world's first **empire**. It stretched from the Persian Gulf to the Mediterranean Sea. The Akkadian empire lasted about 150 years. After its downfall, the Sumerians once again became the most powerful civilization in the region.

> **Who established the world's first empire?**
> _____

RELIGION SHAPES SOCIETY

Religion played an important role in nearly every aspect of Sumerian public and private life. Sumerians practiced **polytheism**, the worship of many gods. Each city-state considered one god to be its special protector. Sumerians believed their gods had enormous powers. Gods could bring a good harvest or a disastrous flood. They could bring illness, or they could bring good health and wealth. The Sumerians believed success in every area of life depended on pleasing the gods. People relied on **priests** to help them gain the gods' favor. Priests had great status. They interpreted the wishes of the gods and made offerings to them.

> **Why did Sumerians try to please the gods?**
> _____
> _____
> _____
> _____

> **Underline the sentence that explains the role of priests in Sumerian society.**

A **social hierarchy** developed in Sumerian city-states. Kings were at the top. They claimed they had been chosen by gods to rule. Below kings were priests and nobles. The middle ranks included skilled craftspeople, merchants, and traders. Farmers and laborers made up the large working class. Slaves were at the bottom of the social order. Although the role of most women was limited to the home and raising children, some upper-class women were educated and even became priestesses.

> **Circle the two groups that formed the Sumerian upper classes.**

INVENTION OF WRITING

The Sumerians made one of the greatest cultural advances in history. They developed **cuneiform** (kyoo-NEE-uh-fohrm), the world's first system of writing. But Sumerians did not have pencils, pens, or paper. Instead, they used sharp reeds, called styluses, to make wedge-shaped symbols on clay tablets. Before cuneiform, written communication used **pictographs**, picture symbols that represented objects. Cuneiform was able to use a variety of symbols that could be combined into one word and express complex ideas and not just objects.

Sumerians first used cuneiform to keep business records, and they would hire a **scribe** to keep track of traded items. They also kept records for the government and temples. Becoming a scribe was a way to move up in social class. Writing was taught in schools. In time, scribes wrote works on law, grammar, and mathematics. Sumerians also wrote stories, proverbs, songs, poems to celebrate military victories, and long poems called **epics**.

ADVANCES AND INVENTIONS

The Sumerians were the first to build wheeled vehicles like carts and wagons. They invented the potter's wheel, a device that spins wet clay as a craftsperson shapes it into bowls. They invented the ox-drawn plow to prepare hard soil for planting, which greatly improved farm production. They built sewers under city streets. They learned to use bronze to make strong tools and weapons, and even invented a clock.

Sumerians developed a math system based on the number 60. From this, they were able to

> Write the name of the world's first system of writing.
>
> _____

> Why were scribes important?
>
> _____
>
> _____
>
> _____

> Which Sumerian invention greatly improved farm production?
>
> _____

Lesson 3, *continued*

INVASIONS OF MESOPOTAMIA

Several other civilizations developed in and around the Fertile Crescent. Their armies battled each other for Mesopotamia's fertile land, and control of the region passed from one empire to another. The Hittites of Asia Minor captured Babylon in 1595 BC, using strong iron weapons and swift **chariots** on the battlefield. Hittite rule did not last long. Their king was killed by an assassin, creating chaos in the kingdom. The Kassites invaded from the north. They captured Babylon and ruled for almost 400 years.

The Assyrians came from northern Mesopotamia and briefly gained control of Babylon in the 1200s BC. They were soon overrun by invaders. However, 300 years later, they began to conquer all of the Fertile Crescent and went as far as Asia Minor and Egypt. The Assyrians had a strong army and were fierce in battle. Anyone who resisted them was killed or harshly punished. They ruled from Nineveh, their own capital city, and demanded taxes across the empire. This required the Assyrians to use local leaders, who governed a small area, collected taxes, enforced laws, and raised troops. The Assyrians also built roads to link distant parts of the empire.

In 612 BC the Chaldeans, a group from the Syrian Desert, conquered the Assyrians and set up their own empire. Nebuchadnezzar (neb-uh-kuhd-NEZ-uhr), the most famous Chaldean king, rebuilt Babylon into a beautiful city. According to legend, his grand palace featured the famous Hanging Gardens. The Chaldeans admired Sumerian culture and made notable advances in astronomy and mathematics.

THE PHOENICIANS

Phoenicia was a wealthy trading society, located at the western end of the Fertile Crescent along the

> Circle the two inventions that helped the Hittites conquer Babylon.

> How did the Assyrians rule their large empire from Nineveh?
>
> _____
> _____
> _____
> _____

> Which older Mesopotamian culture did the Chaldeans admire and study?
>
> _____

Guided Reading Workbook

Mediterranean Sea. Mountains bordered the regions to the north and east. The Phoenicians were mostly urban people. Their chief cities were Tyre, Sidon, and Byblos, port cities that still exist today in the country of Lebanon on the Mediterranean Sea. Phoenicia had few resources other than cedar trees. This wood was a valuable trade item. Since an overland trade route was blocked by mountains, Phoenicians used the sea for trade.

On what body of water were Tyre, Sidon, and Byblos located?
_____ _____

Tyre became one of the best harbors in the world. Fleets of fast Phoenician trading ships sailed throughout the Mediterranean and even as far as the Atlantic Ocean. The Phoenicians built new cities, like Carthage, along their trade routes. They became wealthy by trading cedar wood, silverwork, ivory carvings, glass, and slaves. Purple dye made from shellfish was one of the Phoenicians' most important products. They dyed cloth purple, and it became very popular with rich people around the Mediterranean.

The Phoenicians' most lasting achievement, however, was developing one of the first **alphabets**. It made writing much easier and had a huge impact on the ancient world. The alphabet we use today is based on the Phoenicians'.

Underline the sentence that explains why the Phoenician alphabet had such a lasting effect.

CHALLENGE ACTIVITY

Critical Thinking: Sequence Make a timeline with approximate dates showing the various empires and invasions that characterized the history of Mesopotamia up to the time of the Chaldeans.

vast stretch of desert land to the Mediterranean Sea. The river was so important that Egypt was called the gift of the Nile.

Ancient Egypt developed along a 750-mile stretch of the Nile and included two regions— **Upper Egypt** and **Lower Egypt**. Upper Egypt was the southern region, upriver in relation to the Nile's flow. Lower Egypt was the northern region and was located downriver.

Cataracts, or rapids, marked the southern border of Upper Egypt. In Lower Egypt, the Nile divided into several branches that flowed into the Mediterranean. The branches formed a triangle-shaped **delta**, where soil was deposited by the river. It was a swampy area. Most of Egypt's fertile farmland was in the Nile delta.

> **Where was most of Egypt's farmland located?**
> _____
> _____

Most of Egypt was desert, but rainfall to the south of Egypt would cause the Nile to flood. Almost every year, it would flood Upper Egypt in midsummer and Lower Egypt in the fall. This coated the land around the Nile with rich silt, which made the soil ideal for farming. For Egyptians, the regular floods were a life-giving miracle.

> **Why were yearly floods so important for Egyptians?**
> _____
> _____
> _____

CIVILIZATION DEVELOPS IN EGYPT

Hunter-gatherers first moved to the Nile valley around 12,000 years ago and found plenty of plants, animals, and fish to eat. In time, these people learned how to farm. By 4500 BC farmers were living in villages and growing wheat and barley. They developed an irrigation system to carry water to the fields. Eventually, they were able to raise an abundance of food, including grains, fruits and vegetables, cattle, and sheep. They could also catch geese, ducks, and fish.

> **What does an irrigation system do?**
> _____
> _____

Egypt was protected from invaders by its harsh deserts, the Mediterranean Sea, and the Red Sea. Cataracts made it difficult to sail on the Nile from the south. This helped the villages of Egypt

> **Circle the four natural barriers that protected Egypt from invaders.**

Lesson 4, *continued*

grow. By 3200 BC the villages had organized into two kingdoms with their own rulers. Lower Egypt's capital was Pe, located in the Nile delta. The capital of Upper Egypt was Nekhen, located on the Nile's west bank. For centuries, Egypt was divided into two lands.

KINGS UNIFY EGYPT

According to legend, Menes (MEE-neez), the king of Upper Egypt, invaded Lower Egypt around 3100 BC. He married a princess there in order to unite the two kingdoms under his rule. Menes was the first **pharaoh**, which means ruler of a "great house." He also started the first Egyptian **dynasty**, or series of rulers from the same family. He built a new capital city, Memphis, near where Lower Egypt met Upper Egypt. For centuries, it was the political and cultural center of Egypt. Menes's dynasty, called the First Dynasty, ruled for nearly 200 years. Eventually, rivals challenged the First Dynasty for power and took over Egypt, starting the Second Dynasty.

> What is a dynasty?
> _____
> _____

THE OLD KINGDOM

Around 2700 BC the Third Dynasty began a period in Egyptian history known as the **Old Kingdom**. During the next 500 years, the Egyptians developed a political system based on the belief that the pharaoh was both a king and a god. A government ruled by religious authorities is called a **theocracy**.

> Underline the sentence that defines theocracy.

Although the pharaoh had absolute power over the lands and people, it came with many responsibilities. He was also held personally responsible if anything went wrong. He was blamed if crops did not grow or if there was disease. He was expected to make trade profitable and prevent war.

As the population of Egypt grew, social classes developed. At the top was the pharaoh, with

priests and key government officials making up
the upper class. Many of these people were rich
and powerful **nobles**. The middle class included
lesser government officials, scribes, and rich
craftspeople. Most people, including farmers,
belonged to the lower class. Farmers were often
used by the pharaoh as labor when they did not
work the fields. There were also servants and
slaves for labor.

Trade also developed during the Old Kingdom.
Merchants traveled south along the Nile to
Nubia to acquire gold, copper, ivory, slaves, and
stone. They also traded with Syria for wood. As
society grew more complex, it also became more
disciplined, organized, and highly religious.

> **Circle two countries that Egypt traded with.**

RELIGION AND EGYPTIAN LIFE

The Egyptians practiced polytheism, or the
worship of many gods. During the Old Kingdom,
everyone was expected to worship the same gods,
though the type of worship might be different
from place to place. Egyptians built temples all
over the kingdom. They collected payments from
both worshipers and the government, and the
wealth made them powerful.

> **What is *polytheism*?**
> _____
> _____

Over time, certain cities became centers of
worship for particular gods. In Memphis, for
example, people prayed to Ptah, the creator of
the world. There were, however, many other gods.
Egyptians had a god for nearly everything,
including the sun, sky, and Earth.

Much of Egyptians' religion focused on the
afterlife. They believed the afterlife was a happy
place. Each person had a *ka* (KAH), a spirit or
life force, that left the body after death. However,
it remained linked to the body and could not
leave the burial site. It had to eat, sleep, and be
entertained like a living person. To fulfill the *ka*'s
needs, tombs were filled with furniture, clothing,
tools, jewelry, weapons, and even food and drink.

If the body decayed, the *ka* could not recognize it, which would break the link between body and spirit. So the Egyptians developed a method called embalming to preserve bodies. The bodies were preserved as **mummies**, specially treated bodies wrapped in cloth.

Embalming preserved a body for many years, but it was a complex process that took weeks to complete. The organs were all removed from the body and stored in special jars. The body was then dried out and wrapped in cloths and bandages, often with special charms. Once wrapped, the mummy was placed in a coffin called a sarcophagus. Only royalty and people of wealth and power could afford to be buried as mummies. Poor families buried their dead in shallow graves in the desert, which preserved the bodies naturally.

THE PYRAMIDS

Egyptians believed burial sites were very important. Starting in the Old Kingdom, they built **pyramids** to bury their dead rulers. Pyramids are huge stone structures with a burial chamber deep inside. The largest, the Great Pyramid of Khufu, stands 481 feet (147 m) high.

Many pyramids are still standing today and are amazing examples of Egyptian **engineering**. Historians still are not certain how ancient Egyptians moved the massive stones they needed to build them. A pyramid probably took tens of thousands of workers to build. These workers were paid in grain by the government.

Egyptians believed the pharaoh controlled everyone's afterlife, so they wanted to make his spirit happy with a spectacular pyramid. Pointing to the sky above, the pyramid symbolized the pharaoh's journey to the afterlife. There were often magical spells and hymns on the tomb to keep the pharaoh safe.

> **Why did Egyptians want to preserve bodies by embalming?**
> _____
> _____
> _____

> **What class of people had themselves embalmed as mummies?**
> _____
> _____

> **What question are historians still trying to solve about the pyramids?**
> _____
> _____
> _____

> **Underline the sentence that explains the pointed shape of pyramids.**

Lesson 5, *continued*

Kingdom. It lasted until around 1750 BC when Lower Egypt was conquered by the Hyksos, a people from Southwest Asia. The Hyksos ruled as pharoahs for 200 years until Ahmose of Thebes drove them out in the mid-1500s BC.

Who were the raiders who ended the Middle Kingdom, and where were they from?
_____
_____

THE NEW KINGDOM

Ahmose declared himself king of all Egypt and started the eighteenth dynasty. It was the beginning of the **New Kingdom**, when Egypt reached its height of power and glory.

To prevent invasions like those of the Hyksos, Egypt took control of possible invasion routes. It first took over the Hyksos homeland, then continued north to Syria and as far as the eastern Mediterranean. Next was the kingdom of **Kush**, in Nubia, south of Egypt. By the 1400s BC Egypt was the leading military power in the region. Its empire extended from the Euphrates River to southern Nubia.

Which direction would you go from Egypt to reach Nubia?
_____

Military conquests also made Egypt rich. Conquered kingdoms like Kush sent yearly payments of gold, jewels, and animal skins. Nearby kingdoms like Assyria, Babylon, and the Hittites sent expensive gifts to make sure they had good relations with Egypt. The large empire also expanded Egyptian trade. Profitable **trade routes** were created to distant lands with valuable resources. One ruler in particular, Queen Hatshepsut, was active in sending traders to new lands. She and later pharaohs used the money from trade to create more monuments and temples.

What are two reasons Egypt expanded its trade?
_____
_____
_____

Despite its power, Egypt was threatened by the Hittites from Asia Minor. Pharaoh Ramses the Great fought them fiercely for years, but neither side could defeat the other. Finally, in 1275 BC, both sides signed the Treaty of Kadesh, which historians consider the first peace treaty.

Why did the Egyptians and Hittites sign a peace treaty?
_____
_____

Soon after Ramses died, strong warriors called the Sea People crushed the Hittites and destroyed cities in Southwest Asia. The Egyptians fought them for over 50 years before turning them back. Egypt survived but fell into a period of violence and disorder. The New Kingdom and its empire ended. Egypt would never regain its power.

WORK AND DAILY LIFE

During the Middle and New Kingdoms, Egypt's population continued to grow and become more complex. People took on different trades, which were usually passed on from fathers to sons within families. Professional and skilled workers like scribes, artisans, artists, and architects were honored and admired. These jobs required advanced skills, and many of these people worked for the government and temples.

> **Why would Egyptians want to be a scribe or artisan?**
> _____
> _____

Although trade was important to Egypt, only a small group of people were merchants and traders. Some traveled long distances, and soldiers, scribes, and laborers often went on the trade journeys. Soldiers became more important after the wars of the Middle Kingdom, when Egypt created a permanent army. The military allowed people a chance to improve their social status. They were also paid with land and treasure captured in a war.

> **How were soldiers paid?**
> _____
> _____

For farmers and peasants, who made up most of the population, life never changed. In addition to hard work on the land, they were required to give some of their crop as taxes to the pharaoh. They were also subjected to special labor duty at any time. Only slaves were beneath them in social status. There were few slaves in Egypt, and many were criminals or war prisoners. They had some rights and could earn their freedom.

Family life was important. Most families lived in their own homes. Men were expected to marry young and start families. Women were expected to focus on home and family. Some, though, served as priestesses, royal officials, or artisans. Egyptian women also had legal rights. They could own property, make contracts, and divorce their husbands. Children played games and hunted. Both boys and girls received some education. Schools taught morals, writing, math, and sports. At age 14, most boys entered their father's profession.

> **What legal rights did women have in the Middle and New Kingdoms?**
> _____
> _____
> _____

EGYPTIAN ACHIEVEMENTS

Egyptians invented one of the world's first writing systems, called **hieroglyphics** (hy-ruh-GLIH-fiks). It used more than 600 symbols, mostly pictures of objects. Each symbol represented one or more sounds in the Egyptian language. Hieroglyphics could be written horizontally or vertically, and from either right to left or left to right. This made them difficult to read.

> **Underline the sentence that explains why hieroglyphics were difficult to read.**

At first, hieroglyphics were carved in stone. Later, Egyptians learned how to make a type of paper called **papyrus**. It was made from reeds. Scribes could write on this with brushes and ink. Because papyrus did not decay, many ancient Egyptian texts still survive, including government records, historical records, science texts, medical manuals, and literary works such as *The Book of the Dead*. The discovery of the **Rosetta Stone** in 1799 provided the key to understanding Egyptian writing. The text on the stone slab was written in hieroglyphics and in Greek. Scholars could figure out the hieroglyphics from the Greek words.

> **What language helped scholars to understand the meaning of hieroglyphics on the Rosetta Stone?**
> _____

EGYPTIAN ARCHITECTURE AND ART

Egyptian architects are known not only for the pyramids but also for their magnificent temples.

The temples were lavishly decorated with numerous statues and beautifully painted walls and pillars. **Sphinxes** and **obelisks** were usually found near the entrances to the temples.

Ancient Egyptians were masterful artists, and many of their greatest works are found in either the temples or the tombs of the pharaohs. Most Egyptians, however, never saw these paintings because only kings, priests, or other important people could enter these places.

Egyptian paintings depict a variety of subjects, from crowning kings to religious rituals to scenes from daily life. The paintings also have a particular style. People are drawn showing the sides of their heads and legs, but the fronts of their upper bodies and shoulders are shown straight on. The size of the figure depends on the person's importance in society. Pharaohs are huge and servants are small. In contrast, animals are drawn more realistically. The Egyptians were also skilled stone and metalworkers, creating beautiful statues and jewelry.

Much of what we know about Egyptian art and burial practices comes from the tomb of King Tutankhamen. His tomb was one of the few left untouched by thieves looking for valuables. The tomb was discovered in 1922, and it was filled with treasures.

> **Who were allowed to see ancient Egyptian sculptures and paintings?**
>
> _____
>
> _____
>
> _____

> **Why is King Tutankhamen's tomb so important for the study of Egyptian history?**
>
> _____
>
> _____
>
> _____
>
> _____
>
> _____

CHALLENGE ACTIVITY

Critical Thinking: Interpret Using the library or an online resource, find a key for translating Egyptian hieroglyphics into English. Write a short message using hieroglyphics and trade with another student to see if you can read each other's messages. Give a copy of your message and the translation to your teacher.

Early Civilizations of the Fertile Crescent and the Nile Valley

Lesson 6

MAIN IDEAS
1. Geography helped early Kush civilization develop in Nubia.
2. Kush and Egypt traded, but they also fought.
3. Later, Kush became a trading power with a unique culture.
4. Both internal and external factors led to the decline of Kush.

Key Terms and Places

Nubia region in northeast Africa where the kingdom of Kush developed

ebony type of dark, heavy wood

ivory white material taken from elephant tusks

Meroë economic center of Kush; last Kushite capital

trade network system of people in different lands who trade goods back and forth

merchants traders

exports items sent to other regions for trade

imports goods brought in from other regions

Lesson Summary
GEOGRAPHY AND EARLY KUSH

The kingdom of Kush developed south of Egypt along the Nile, in the region we now call **Nubia**. It was the first large kingdom in the interior of Africa. Every year, floods from the Nile provided a rich layer of fertile soil. Farmers planted grains and other crops. The area was also rich in minerals such as gold, copper, and stone. These resources contributed to the region's wealth.

Over time, some rich farmers became leaders of their villages. Around 2000 BC one of these leaders took control of other villages and made himself king of Kush. The kings of Kush ruled from their capital at Kerma (KAR-muh). The city was located on the Nile just south of a cataract, or stretch of rapids. Because the Nile's cataracts made parts of the river hard to pass through,

> What valuable minerals were important to Kush's prosperity?
> _____

> Around what year did the first king of Kush appear?
> _____

they were natural barriers to the powerful
Egyptians in the north.

As time passed, Kushite society became more
complex. In addition to farmers and herders,
some people of Kush became priests or artisans.

How did the Nile's cataracts protect the Kush?
_____
_____

KUSH AND EGYPT

Kush and Egypt were neighbors and trading
partners. The Kushites sent gold, copper, and
stone to Egypt, as well as prized materials such as
dark **ebony** wood and **ivory** tusks from elephants.
They also sent slaves to be servants or soldiers for
the pharaoh.

Relations between Kush and Egypt were not
always peaceful, however. As Kush grew rich and
more powerful, the Egyptians feared Kush would
attack them. Around 1500 BC Egyptian armies
under the pharaoh Thutmose I invaded and
conquered northern Nubia, including all of
Kush. Thutmose destroyed the Kushite palace at
Kerma. Kush remained an Egyptian territory for
450 years. During that time, Egypt influenced the
language, culture, and religion of Kush.

Why did Egypt invade Kush?
_____
_____

In the mid-1000s BC, when Egypt's New
Kingdom was ending, Kushite leaders regained
control. Kush once again became independent.
By around 850 BC Kush was as strong as it had
been before it was conquered by Egypt. During
the 700s BC, under the king Kashta, Kush
attacked Egypt. By 751 BC he had conquered
Upper Egypt and established relations with
Lower Egypt. After Kashta died, his son Piankhi
(PYANG-kee) continued to attack Egypt. He
believed the gods wanted him to rule all of
Egypt. By the time he died in 716 BC, Piankhi
had accomplished this task. His kingdom
extended north from Kush's capital of Napata all
the way to the Nile delta.

Underline the sentence that explains why Piankhi continued to attack Egypt after his father's death.

Piankhi's brother, Shabaka (SHAB-uh-kuh),
declared himself pharaoh and began the

Twenty-fifth, or Kushite, Dynasty in Egypt. Egyptian culture thrived during the Kushite Dynasty, which remained strong for about 40 years. In the 670s BC, however, Egypt was invaded by the Assyrians from Mesopotamia. The Assyrians' iron weapons were better than the Kushites' bronze weapons. The Kushites were driven completely out of Egypt in just ten years.

How were Assyrian weapons different from Kushite weapons?
_____
_____
_____

LATER KUSH

After they lost control of Egypt, the people of Kush devoted themselves to increasing agriculture and trade. They hoped to make their country rich again and succeeded within a few centuries. The new capital, **Meroë** (MER-oh-wee), was the economic center of Kush. Gold could be found nearby, as could forests of ebony and other wood. The area was also rich in iron ore, and the Kushites quickly developed an iron industry.

What industry helped make Kush a rich and successful kingdom again?
_____

Meroë was located on the Nile, and it became the center of a large **trade network**. The Kushites sent goods down the Nile to Egypt. From there, Egyptian and Greek **merchants** carried goods to ports on the Mediterranean and Red Seas and to southern Africa. These goods may have eventually reached India and perhaps China. Kush's **exports** included gold, pottery, iron tools, ivory, leopard skins, ostrich feathers, elephants, and slaves. **Imports** included jewelry and luxury items from Egypt, Asia, and lands along the Mediterranean.

What direction is "down the Nile"?
_____

Kushite merchants brought back customs from many cultures, but Egypt was the most obvious influence on Kush's culture during this period. However, many elements of Kushite culture were not borrowed from anywhere else. Although many Kushites worshiped Egyptian gods, they also worshiped their own gods. They also developed their own written language.

Circle two elements of Kushite culture that were unique to them.

Women were expected to be active in their society. They worked alongside men in the fields, as well as raised children and performed household tasks. Many women fought during wars. Women could rise to positions of great authority, especially in religion. Some rulers made princesses in their families powerful priestesses. Some women were co-rulers with their husbands or sons. A few women, such as Queen Shanakhdakheto (shah-nahk-dah-KEE-toh), even ruled the empire alone and helped increase the strength and wealth of the kingdom.

> How were the roles of Kushite women different from most other ancient civilizations?
>
> _____
> _____
> _____
> _____
> _____

DECLINE AND DEFEAT

Kushite civilization centered at Meroë reached its height in the first century BC. However, after four centuries, it fell due to both external and internal factors. It is possible that farmers overgrazed cattle, so that the soil could no longer be farmed. Also, ironmakers probably used up the forests where they got wood to fire their iron furnaces. Kush could no longer produce enough weapons for its army or trade goods for its economy.

> Underline the text that explains how the iron industry might have helped cause the fall of Kush.

Trade routes started going around Kush to another powerful trading center, Aksum (AHK-soom). Aksum was located southeast of Kush on the Red Sea, where Ethiopia and Eritrea are today. As Kush declined, Aksum became the most powerful state in the region. About AD 350 the Aksumite leader King Ezana (AY-zah-nah) sent an invading army and conquered the once-powerful Kush. In the late 300s Aksum's rulers became Christian. The new religion reshaped Nubian culture, and Kush's influence disappeared.

> Circle the name and kindgom of the ruler who eventually defeated Kush.

World Religions of Southwest Asia

MAIN IDEAS

1. The Jews' early history began in Canaan and ended when the Romans forced them out of Israel.
2. Jewish beliefs in God, justice, and law anchor their society.
3. Jewish sacred texts describe the laws and principles of Judaism.
4. Traditions and holy days celebrate the history and religion of the Jewish people.

Key Terms and Places

Judaism Hebrews' religion

Canaan land where Abraham settled by the Mediterranean Sea

Exodus journey of the Hebrews out of Egypt, led by Moses

rabbis religious teachers of Judaism

monotheism belief in one and only one God

Torah most sacred text of Judaism

Lesson Summary

EARLY HISTORY

The Hebrews appeared in Southwest Asia sometime between 2000 and 1500 BC. Their religion was **Judaism**. Some of their early history was written by Hebrew scribes. These accounts became the Hebrew Bible. The Bible says that the Hebrews started with a man named Abraham. According to the Bible, God told Abraham to leave Mesopotamia and go to the land of **Canaan** on the Mediterranean Sea. God promised that Abraham's descendants would become a mighty nation.

Some of Abraham's descendants, the Israelites, lived in Canaan for many years. Later, a famine caused some to move to Egypt. They prospered there. Egypt's pharaoh feared that the Israelites would become too powerful, so he made them slaves. According to the Bible, a leader named Moses freed the Israelites and led them out of Egypt. During this long journey, called the

Circle the name of the man who the Bible says is the first Hebrew.

Why did some Israelites move to Egypt?

_____

_____

Exodus, God is said to have given Moses two stone tablets on a mountain called Sinai. A code of moral laws called the Ten Commandments was written on the tablets.

The Israelites reached Canaan, or Israel, but in the mid-1000s BC, invaders swept through the land. Strong kings like David and Solomon kept the country together and expanded its territory. It grew rich through trade, and Solomon built a great temple in Jerusalem.

Eventually, conflict split Israel into two kingdoms—Israel and Judah. The people of Judah became known as Jews. The two kingdoms lasted for a few centuries until they fell to invaders. When Judah fell in 586 BC, the Jews were sent from Jerusalem as slaves. When the invaders were conquered, some Jews returned home. Some moved to other places. This scattering of Jews outside of Israel and Judah is called the Diaspora.

The Jews ruled themselves for about 100 years, but then the Romans conquered them. The Jews rebelled and the Romans punished them. The great temple was destroyed. Many people were killed or enslaved, and thousands fled Jerusalem. Over the next centuries, Jews moved around the world, where they often faced discrimination from other religious groups.

After the temple was destroyed, roles in society changed. The role of a priest was no longer as important for religious practices. Instead, **rabbis,** or religious teachers, became more important as the Jews spread across the world. Even before the temple was destroyed, women could not become priests or rabbis. Men made most decisions. Women's husbands were chosen by the woman's father, and family property went to the eldest son.

> Who were the kings who saved Israel and made it rich?
> _____
> _____

> What is the Diaspora?
> _____
> _____
> _____

> Underline the sentence that explains why rabbis replaced priests as the most important religious figures.

JEWISH BELIEFS

No matter where they live, Jews base their society on Jewish beliefs. Their most important belief is that there is one, and only one, God. This is known as **monotheism.** Most ancient cultures worshipped many gods, so the Jews' belief set them apart. Also central to Jewish religion are the ideas of justice and righteousness. *Justice* means kindness and fairness toward all: to the poor, sick, and even strangers and criminals. *Righteousness* means doing what is right, even if others do not. Jews value righteousness over rituals.

Jews believe their religious laws were given to them by God. The most important laws are the Ten Commandments, which are still followed by many people today. The Jews also follow laws, called Mosaic laws, that guide their daily lives. These rules explain how people worship and even what foods they eat. Foods that are allowed and prepared according to these laws are called kosher.

> **Underline the definition of *monotheism*.**

> **What are the most important laws for the Jewish people?**
> _____

JEWISH TEXTS

Judaism has several sacred texts. These contain the religion's basic laws and principles. The **Torah,** the first five books of the Hebrew Bible, is the most sacred text. It is central to Jewish religious services. The Hebrew Bible has two other parts besides the Torah. The second is the writing of Hebrew prophets, people who were believed to receive messages from God. The final part has poetry, songs, stories, lessons, and history. Many of these stories show the power of faith.

The Talmud is a collection of commentaries written by rabbis and scholars over the centuries. The commentaries explain the Torah and Jewish law. Most were written between AD 200 and 600.

> **What are the three parts of the Hebrew Bible?**
> _____
> _____
> _____
> _____

They are second only to the Hebrew Bible in importance.

TRADITIONS AND HOLY DAYS

The Jewish holiday Hanukkah falls in December. It honors a historical event. The Jews wanted to celebrate a victory that had convinced their rulers to let them keep their religion. According to legend, the Jews did not have enough lamp oil to celebrate at the temple. But somehow the oil they had, enough for one day, burned for eight days. So Jews today celebrate by lighting candles for eight days. More important is the holiday of Passover, celebrated in March or April. It honors the Exodus from Egypt. During this holiday, Jews eat a flat, unrisen bread called matzo.

> Circle the type of bread eaten during Passover.

The two most sacred Jewish holidays are called the High Holy Days. These take place in September or October. The first two days of celebration are Rosh Hashanah, which is the start of the new year in the Jewish calendar. Yom Kippur comes shortly after. It is the holiest day of the year for Jews. On this day, Jews ask God to forgive their sins. They pray and do not eat or drink. They reflect on the past year and resolve to improve.

> What is the holiest day of the year for Jews?
> _____

CHALLENGE ACTIVITY

Critical Thinking: Draw Conclusions Imagine you are helping to plan a museum of ancient Jewish history. Write a brief recommendation for three exhibits you would like to include.

By the time Jesus was about 30, he began to travel and teach.

Jesus had many followers, but his teachings challenged political and religious leaders. They arrested him while he was in Jerusalem around AD 30. Shortly after his arrest, the Romans tried and executed Jesus. He was nailed to a cross, which is called crucifixion. After he died, his followers buried him. According to the Bible, Jesus rose from the dead three days later. This event is known as the **Resurrection.** He then appeared to his **disciples,** or followers. He gave them instructions about how to pass on his teachings. Then he rose up to Heaven.

Early Christians believed that the Resurrection was a sign that Jesus was the Messiah and the son of God. They called him Jesus Christ from the Greek word for Messiah, *Christos.*

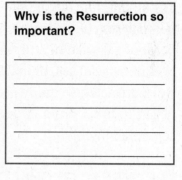

Why is the Resurrection so important?

_____

_____

_____

_____

_____

JESUS' ACTS AND TEACHINGS

During his life, Jesus traveled from village to village, spreading his message. Many people became followers after they saw him perform miracles. He also told many parables, or stories that taught lessons about how people should live. He explained complicated ideas in ways most people could understand. Jesus taught people to love God and love all people, two rules from the Torah. Jesus also taught about salvation, or the rescue of people from sin.

Since Jesus' death, people have interpreted his teachings in different ways. As a result, different denominations, or groups, of Christianity have developed.

Underline three of Jesus' major teachings.

JESUS' FOLLOWERS

After Jesus' death, his followers continued to spread his teachings. The 12 disciples who knew him best were called the Apostles. One of them, Peter, traveled as far as Rome to teach people about Jesus. He is often thought of as the first leader of the Christian Church. The disciples Matthew, Mark, Luke, and John wrote accounts of Jesus' life and teachings. These accounts are called the Gospels. They are in the New Testament.

Probably the most important person involved in spreading Christianity was Paul of Tarsus. Christians regard Paul as a **saint.** A saint is a person known and admired for his or her holiness. Paul never met Jesus and at first opposed the Christians. According to the New Testament, one day he saw a blinding light and heard Jesus calling out to him. After that, he became a Christian and traveled around the Mediterranean teaching Christian beliefs. His work attracted so many people that Christianity began to break from its Jewish roots. It became a separate religion.

What are the Gospels?

_____
_____
_____
_____

Why do you think Paul is important to Christians?

_____
_____

THE SPREAD OF CHRISTIANITY

Christianity spread quickly in Roman communities. Some Roman leaders wanted to put an end to the new religion. They arrested and killed Christians who refused to worship the gods of Rome. By the 200s and 300s, some emperors feared Christians could cause unrest. They banned Christian worship.

Christians continued to meet in secret. This made it hard to have a single leader. Instead, local leaders called bishops led each Christian community. Christians looked to the bishops in large cities for guidance. Eventually, the bishop of Rome, or the pope, came to be viewed as the head of the whole Christian Church. Women had been leaders in early Christian communities, but they were not allowed to be bishops or popes as Christianity became more established.

Christianity continued to spread throughout Rome. Then the Roman emperor Constantine

What did the first bishops do?

_____
_____
_____

Circle the name for the bishop of Rome.

Other Arabs led a settled life. They lived in oases where they could farm. Towns sprang up in oases along the trade routes. There, nomads could trade animal products for supplies. Merchants came in caravans to sell goods like spices, gold, and leather.

A NEW RELIGION

In early times, Arabs worshipped many gods. That changed when a man named Muhammad brought a new religion to Arabia. Most of what we know about him comes from religious writings. Muhammad was born in the city of **Mecca** around 570. As a child, he traveled with his uncle's caravans. As an adult, Muhammad managed a caravan business owned by his wife Khadijah.

> Circle the name of the city where Muhammad was born.

Trade made Mecca a rich city, but most of the wealth belonged to a few people. Muhammad was upset that rich people did not help the poor. He often went to a cave to pray and meditate on this problem. According to Islamic writings, when Muhammad was 40, an angel spoke to him. The angel told him the words of God. Muhammad was God's prophet, and he would tell God's messages to the world. These messages form the basis of the religion called **Islam,** which means "to submit to God" in Arabic. A follower of Islam is called a **Muslim.** The messages were collected in the **Qur´an** (kuh-RAN), the holy book of Islam.

> What problem troubled Muhammad?
>
> _____
>
> _____
>
> _____

In 613, Muhammad began to spread his message. He taught that there was only one God, Allah, which means "the God" in Arabic. Like Judaism and Christianity, Islam is monotheistic, believing in one God. However, their beliefs about God are not the same. Muhammad also taught that all people who believed in Allah should be like family. Like in families, people with money should help people who are less fortunate.

> What does Islam have in common with Judaism and Christianity?
>
> _____
>
> _____
>
> _____

Guided Reading Workbook

Slowly, Muhammad got more followers. As Islam spread, Mecca's rulers grew worried. They planned to kill Muhammed. In 622 Muhammed and his followers moved to **Medina,** which means "the Prophet's city" in Arabic. His departure from Mecca is called the hegira, or journey. It is such an important event that Muslims made 622 the first year of the Islamic calendar.

Muhammad became a spiritual and political leader in Medina. His house became the first **mosque,** a building for worship and prayer. More Arab tribes began to accept Islam. After some years of fighting, the people of Mecca also became Muslim. By the time Muhammad died in 632, Islam was practiced by most people in Arabia. Over the centuries, it spread throughout the world.

What is the hegira?
_____
_____
_____

THE QUR´AN

After Muhammad died, his followers wrote down all his teachings to form the book known as the Qur´an. Muslims believe that the Qur´an is the exact word of God as it was told to Muhammad. The Qur´an says there is one God—Allah—and that Muhammad is his prophet. Muslims must obey Allah's commands, which they learned from Muhammad.

Underline the sentence that explains what Muslims believe about the words in the Qur´an.

Islam teaches that there is a definite beginning and end to the world. On that final day, Muslims believe, God will judge all people. Those who have obeyed God's orders will go to paradise. Those who have not obeyed God will be punished.

The Qur´an also gives rules that guide the everyday life of Muslims. These include rules about worship, moral behavior, social life, and what Muslims can eat and drink. For example, Muslims cannot eat pork or drink alcohol. Some rules are not stated directly in the Qur´an,

According to the Qur´an, what will happen at the end of the world?
_____
_____
_____
_____
_____

but Muslims still use it as a guide. Before
Muhammad, many Arabs owned slaves, but
many Muslims chose to free their slaves based on
the teachings of the Qur´an.

Women's rights were also described in the
Qur´an. Like other societies at that time, women
had fewer rights than men. However, they could
own property, earn money, and get an education.

Jihad (ji-HAHD) is an important subject in the
Qur´an. Jihad means "to make an effort" or
"to struggle." It refers to the internal struggle of
a Muslim trying to obey God and follow Islamic
beliefs. It can also mean the struggle to defend
the Muslim community or, historically, to convert
people to Islam. The word has also been
translated as "holy war."

> Circle the two meanings
> of jihad.

THE SUNNAH

Besides the Qur´an, Muslims also study the
hadith. This is the written record of
Muhammad's words and actions. It is the basis
for the **Sunnah** (SOOH-nuh). The Sunnah refers
to the way Muhammad lived, which is a model
for how Muslims should behave.

> What is the hadith?
> _____
> _____
> _____
> _____

The Sunnah explains five acts of worship
required of all Muslims. These are known as the
Five Pillars of Islam. The *first pillar* is a statement
of faith that Muslims must say at least once in
their lives: "There is no god but God, and
Muhammad is his prophet." The *second pillar*
says a Muslim must pray five times daily. The
third pillar is a yearly donation to charity. The
fourth pillar is fasting during the holy month of
Ramadan (RAH-muh-dahn). The Qur´an says
that this is the month that Muhammad first
received the word of God. During that month,
Muslims will not eat or drink anything between
dawn and dusk. This shows that God is more
important than one's own body. It also reminds
Muslims of people who struggle to get enough

> What is the fourth pillar,
> and why is it important to
> Muslims?
> _____
> _____
> _____
> _____
> _____

Lesson 3, *continued*

food. The *fifth pillar* is the hajj (HAJ), a pilgrimage to Mecca. The Kaaba in Mecca is Islam's most sacred place. Muslims must try to go to Mecca at least once in their lifetime.

The Sunnah also preaches moral duties that must be met in daily life, in business, and in government. One rule says that it is bad to owe someone money. There are also rules about lending money and charging interest. This has affected the economies of Muslim countries. Many people would not use banks. Today, banking is more common because of the global economy.

> Underline the sentence that explains what parts of Muslim life are affected by the Sunnah.

ISLAMIC LAW

The Qur'an and the Sunnah form the basis of Islamic law, or Shariah (shuh-REE-uh). Shariah uses both Islamic sources and human reason to judge a person's actions. Actions fall on a scale ranging from required to accepted to disapproved to forbidden. Shariah sets rewards for good behavior and punishments for crimes. It also sets limits on authority. It was the basis for law in Muslim countries until modern times. Today, most Islamic countries blend Islamic law with a legal system much like that in the United States.

> Describe the system of laws used in most Islamic nations today.
>
> _____
> _____
> _____
> _____

CHALLENGE ACTIVITY

Critical Thinking: Draw Inferences Why might it be helpful to have Five Pillars, or main duties, to perform?

The region's main landforms are rivers, plains, plateaus, and mountains. Its two major rivers are the **Tigris** and **Euphrates** in Iraq. They join together before they reach the Persian Gulf. They are called exotic rivers because they start in wet regions and flow through dry areas. The rivers create a narrow fertile area, which was called Mesopotamia in ancient times.

> **What country has two exotic rivers flowing through it?**
>
> _____

The Arabian Peninsula has no permanent rivers. It is covered with vast dry plains in the east. These desert plains are covered with sand in the south and volcanic rock in the north. The landscape rises as the peninsula reaches the Red Sea. It becomes mountains and plateaus. The mountains of Yemen are the highest point.

> **Underline the sentence that explains where the highest point is on the Arabian Peninsula.**

Plateaus and mountains also cover most of Iran. Iran is one of the world's most mountainous countries. The Zagros Mountains are in the west. The Elburz Mountains and the Kopet-Dag lie in the north.

The region's desert climate can get very hot in the day and very cold at night. Southern Saudi Arabia has the world's largest sand desert, the Rub al Khali. Its name means "Empty Quarter" because it has so little life. In northern Saudi Arabia, there is another large desert called An Nafud. These deserts are among the driest places in the world.

> **Why is Rub al Khali called the Empty Quarter?**
>
> _____
>
> _____

Some areas with plateaus and mountains get rain or winter snow. They usually have semiarid steppe climates and may get more than 50 inches of rain a year. Trees grow in these areas. Plants may also grow in **oases** in the desert. At an oasis, underground water bubbles up to the surface. Most desert plants grow without much water. Their roots either go very deep or spread out very far to get as much water as they can.

Water is one of this region's two most valuable resources. But water is scarce. Some places in the desert have springs that give water. Wells also provide water. Some wells are dug into dry streambeds called **wadis.** Modern wells can go very deep underground to get **fossil water.** This is water that is not replaced by rain, so these wells will run dry over time.

Oil is the region's other important resource. This resource is plentiful. Oil has brought great wealth to the countries that have oil fields. Most oil fields are near the shores of the Persian Gulf. But oil cannot be replaced once it is taken. Too much drilling for oil now may cause economic problems in the future.

Circle the most important resources in this region.

CENTRAL ASIA

Central Asia is in the middle of Asia. Its physical geography includes rugged terrain that has isolated the region. All the countries in this region are **landlocked.** That means they are surrounded by land, with no access to the ocean.

In the south, the high Hindu Kush mountains stretch through Afghanistan. In the east, Tajikistan and Kyrgyzstan are also very mountainous. High mountains, such as the **Pamirs,** have glaciers. Through history, the mountains have made communication and travel difficult.

What two factors make Central Asia isolated?
_____
_____

From the mountains, the land slowly slopes down to the Caspian Sea in the west. Some land there is 95 feet (29 m) below sea level. Between the sea and mountains are plains and low plateaus. The fertile **Fergana Valley** is in the plains. It has been a center of farming for thousands of years. Two rivers flow through it: the Syr Darya and the Amu Darya. They flow from the eastern mountains into the **Aral Sea,** which is really a large lake. Lake Balkhash is also

Circle the name of the sea that is really a large lake.

The Arabian Peninsula to Central Asia

> **MAIN IDEAS**
> 1. Islamic culture and an economy greatly based on oil influence life in Saudi Arabia.
> 2. Most Arabian Peninsula countries other than Iraq and Iran are monarchies influenced by Islamic culture and oil resources.

Key Terms and Places

Islam religion founded by Muhammad around AD 622 in Arabia

Shia branch of Islam in which Muslims believe that true interpretations of Islamic teachings can only come from certain religious and political leaders

Sunni branch of Islam in which Muslims believe in the ability of the majority of the community to interpret Islamic teachings

OPEC Organization of Petroleum Exporting Countries, an international organization whose members work to influence the price of oil on world markets by controlling the supply

quota number or value limit on goods

Lesson Summary
SAUDI ARABIA

Saudi Arabia is the largest country on the Arabian Peninsula. It is a major center of religion and culture, and it has one of the region's strongest economies. Most Saudis speak Arabic. Their culture and customs are strongly influenced by **Islam.**

Islam began in Arabia, and it is based on the messages that Muslims believe Muhammad received from God around AD 622. The messages are written in the Qur´an. Most Saudis follow one of two branches of Islam. **Shia** Muslims believe that only certain imams—religious and political leaders—can interpret Islamic teaching. About 85–90 percent of Saudi Muslims are **Sunni.** They believe Islam can be interpreted by the community.

> **What is the main language in Saudi Arabia?**
> _____

> **What branch of Islam do most Saudis follow?**
> _____

Islam influences Saudi laws and customs in many ways. It teaches modesty, so traditional clothing is long and loose, covering the arms and legs. Women usually wear a black cloak and veil in public, though some wear Western-style clothing. Few go out in public without a husband or male relative with them. However, women can own and run businesses. In 2015 women were given the right to vote, and by June of 2018 they will be allowed to drive.

> **When were Saudi women first allowed to vote?**
> _____

Saudi Arabia's government is a monarchy. The Saud family has ruled the country since 1932. Most government officials are relatives of the king. However, local officials are elected.

Oil is one of the most important influences on Saudi Arabia's economy and foreign policy. The country has almost one-fifth of the world's oil. It exports the most oil. This makes Saudi Arabia an important member of **OPEC,** the Organization of the Petroleum Exporting Countries.

> **Why is Saudi Arabia such an important member of OPEC?**
> _____
> _____
> _____

OPEC has members from many countries. It controls the supply of oil, which affects the price of oil around the world. The organization places a **quota,** or limit, on each member nation. No OPEC member can produce and export more oil than the quota value it is allowed.

Money from oil has helped Saudi Arabia build roads, schools, hospitals, and universities. This has helped create a large middle class. Its people also have free health care and education. However, there are also challenges. There are few industries besides oil, which will run out one day. About one quarter of young Saudis are unemployed because there are not many opportunities for work.

> **Underline the sentence that explains why Saudi Arabia may have economic problems in the future.**

Saudi Arabia has created programs to fight unemployment and encourage economic growth. It is trying to make it easier for people to start their own small businesses and to give support to entrepreneurs. It is also making changes to its

> **Why does Saudi Arabia need to find new ways to grow food?**
> _____
> _____
> _____

agricultural and water policies. Because it has few water resources, the country is studying new ways to grow enough food for its population without losing too much of its underground water.

OTHER COUNTRIES OF THE ARABIAN PENINSULA

There are six smaller countries in this region: Kuwait, Bahrain, Qatar, the United Arab Emirates (UAE), Oman, and Yemen. Like Saudi Arabia, they are all influenced by Islam. Most have monarchies and depend on oil.

Oil was discovered in Kuwait in the 1930s. It made the country very rich. In 1990 Iraq invaded Kuwait to gain control of Kuwaiti oil. This started the Persian Gulf War. The United States and other countries defeated Iraq, but the war destroyed many of Kuwait's oil fields.

Kuwait's government is a monarchy, but the country elected a legislature in 1992. Until 2005, only about 15 percent of Kuwait's men were allowed to vote. In 2005 women were given the right to vote.

Bahrain is a group of islands in the Persian Gulf. It has a powerful monarchy with a legislature. Oil made Bahrain wealthy. Most people there live in big, modern cities. In the 1990s the country began to run out of oil. Now banking and tourism are major industries.

Qatar is located on a small peninsula in the Persian Gulf. Its economy is based on oil and natural gas, which have made it rich. Qatar has a powerful monarch. However, in 2003 the people voted to approve a new constitution. It gave more power to elected officials.

The United Arab Emirates, or UAE, is seven tiny kingdoms. People there have a modern, comfortable lifestyle because of profits from oil and natural gas. It has more foreign workers than citizens because it has such a small population.

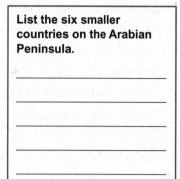

List the six smaller countries on the Arabian Peninsula.
_____
_____
_____
_____
_____
_____

Circle three ways besides oil that countries in this region are supporting their economies.

Why does the UAE have more foreign workers than citizens?
_____
_____

Oman covers most of the southeastern part of the Arabian Peninsula. Though its economy is also based on oil, it is not as rich as Kuwait or the UAE. The government is trying to create new industries such as tourism and manufacturing.

Yemen is in the southwestern part of the Arabian Peninsula. Its government is elected, but it suffers from corruption. Oil was discovered in Yemen in the 1980s. Even though oil and coffee created income for the country, it is still the poorest on the Arabian Peninsula.

A civil war has caused many problems in the country. Forces loyal to the government are fighting rebel movements. Citizens cannot get the food and fuel they need. About two million people have either left their homes or fled the country. The United Nations is working to end the conflict.

> **What problems has the civil war caused Yemen's people?**
>
> _____
>
> _____
>
> _____

CHALLENGE ACTIVITY

Critical Thinking: Compare and Contrast Use a Venn diagram or a Features Chart to compare and contrast Saudi Arabia with at least two other countries of the Arabian Peninsula. Consider features such as religious influences, resources, governments, and economies.

forced Iraq from Kuwait. This was called the Persian Gulf War, and it lasted six weeks. After the war, Saddam Hussein did not accept all the terms of peace, so the United Nations placed an **embargo,** or trade limit, on Iraq. This hurt the economy.

Soon after, Shia Muslims and Kurds rebelled against Saddam. He brutally put down these uprisings. The UN forced Iraq to end all military activity and sent inspectors to make sure Saddam destroyed all weapons of mass destruction. Iraq refused to cooperate.

The terrorist attacks on U.S. soil on September 11, 2001, led to more tension between the United States and Iraq. In March 2003 the United States invaded Iraq and defeated the Iraqi army in a few weeks. Saddam Hussein went into hiding, and Iraq's government fell. When he was found, Saddam Hussein was arrested, tried, and executed for his crimes.

PEOPLE AND CULTURE

Iraq has about 38 million people and is about the size of California. Most Iraqis live in cities. They belong to two major ethnic groups: Arabs and Kurds. Arabs make up 75 to 80 percent of Iraq's population. They speak Arabic, the country's official language. The Kurds speak Kurdish as well as Arabic. Kurds are mostly farmers and live in a large region in the north of Iraq.

Most Iraqis are Muslim, and religion plays a large role in their lives. The two branches of Islam—Shia and Sunni—are practiced. About 60 to 65 percent of Iraqis are Shia Muslims and live in the south. About one third are Sunni Muslims and live in the north. Most Kurds identify as Muslims, but they practice a variety of religions and are known for their religious tolerance.

> **Why did the UN place an embargo on Iraq?**
> _____
> _____
> _____
> _____

> **When did the United States invade Iraq?**
> _____

> **Circle the names of Iraq's two ethnic groups.**

> **What branch of Islam is practiced by the majority of Iraqis?**
> _____

IRAQ TODAY

Today, Iraq is slowly recovering from war, though there is still fighting and violence. **Baghdad,** Iraq's capital of 6 million people, was badly damaged. People lost electricity and running water. After the war, the U.S. military and private companies helped to restore water and electricity and to rebuild homes, businesses, and schools.

In January 2005 the people of Iraq took part in democracy for the first time. Millions voted for members of the National Assembly. This group's main task was to write Iraq's new constitution. However, conflicts between groups made it difficult to have a stable government.

Iraq is trying to rebuild a strong economy. The country was once the world's second-largest oil exporter, but it is not clear if they can restore that level of oil production. Crops like barley, cotton, and rice are also important resources.

Iraq's future remains uncertain. Although there has been some progress building a new elected government, it remains weak and corrupt. Poverty is widespread and there are many refugees. A violent Sunni Muslim militant group called the Islamic State and the Levant (ISIL) has committed acts of terror across the globe and ethnic cleansing in Iraq. They want to create a state that supports an extreme form of Islam. U.S. military advisors returned to Iraq in 2014. However, the threat of ISIL and Iraq's weak government continue to be a challenge for the country and the rest of the world.

> In 2015 the population of the city of Los Angeles was almost 4 million people. How does this compare to Baghdad's population?
>
> _____
> _____
> _____

> Underline the sentence that describes Iraq's important resources other than oil.

> Name four reasons that Iraq is having trouble rebuilding.
>
> _____
> _____
> _____
> _____

traditions. Trade made the Safavids wealthy and they built glorious mosques in their capital **Esfahan.**

In 1921 the Persian title of shah was again taken. This time it was claimed by an Iranian military officer who took power. In 1941 his son took control. This shah was an ally of the United States and Britain. He tried to make Iran more modern, but his programs were not popular.

In 1978 Iranians began a **revolution.** By 1979 they overthrew the shah and set up an Islamic republic. This type of government follows strict Islamic law. Soon after the revolution began, Iran's relations with the United States broke down. A mob of students attacked the U.S. Embassy in **Tehran,** Iran's capital. Over 50 Americans were held hostage for a year, with the approval of Iran's government.

> Underline the phrase that explains what an Islamic republic does.

IRAN TODAY

In Southwest Asia most people are Arabs and speak Arabic. In Iran, however, more than half the people are Persian. They speak Farsi, the Persian language.

Iran has one of Southwest Asia's largest populations. It has about 83 million people, and the average age is about 29. It is ethnically diverse. Along with Persians, there are Azeris, Lurs, Kurds, Arabs, and Turks. Most Iranians are Shia Muslim. About 5 to 10 percent are Sunni Muslim. Others practice Christianity, Judaism, and other religions.

> How is Iranian culture different from other Southwest Asian cultures?
>
> _____
> _____
> _____

In addition to Islamic holy days, Iranians celebrate Nowruz, the Persian New Year. The culture centers on families, and Persian food is important at family gatherings. Meat is especially significant during holidays. It also is associated with upper-class meals, so it has social significance. However, raising animals for food is an environmental problem in a country where land and water use must be limited.

Iran's huge oil reserves have made it wealthy. The country is also known for its beautiful woven carpets. Agriculture is also important to the economy, employing about one-third of Iran's workforce. The younger population is finding jobs in a growing technology sector. Technology is considered a national priority, and many university graduates have science and engineering degrees. Entrepreneurs are also creating new businesses.

> **Circle three occupations that employ Iran's workforce.**

Iran's government is a **theocracy.** Its rulers, or *ayatollahs,* are religious leaders with unlimited power. The country also has an elected president and parliament. Iran's government has supported many hard-line policies, such as terrorism. In 1997, there were signs that it might adopt some democratic reforms that would improve Iran's economy and women's rights.

> **What is an *ayatollah*?**
> _____
> _____
> _____

In 2005 and 2009, however, Iranians elected a president who wanted Iranians to follow strict Islamic law. He lost supporters when his government was accused of corruption and mismanagement. A new president was elected in 2013.

Today, the United States and other nations are concerned about Iran's nuclear program as a threat to world security. The United Nations imposed sanctions, or penalties, on Iran. These were reduced by several countries when Iran confirmed that it had scaled back its nuclear activities.

> **What activity in Iran is causing concern for the United States and other nations?**
> _____

The Silk Road brought many people into Central Asia. In AD 500 Turkic-speaking nomads came from northern Asia. In the 700s Arabs conquered the region. They brought their religion, Islam. The Mongols took over in the 1200s. When their empire fell, groups such as the Uzbeks, Kazaks, and Turkmen came in.

> **Circle the dates that the Arabs and Mongols conquered Central Asia.**

In the mid-1800s Russia conquered this region. Russians built railroads and increased oil and cotton production. But people began to resist Russia's rule. After the Soviets took power in Russia, they wanted to weaken resistance to their rule. So they divided Central Asia into republics. They encouraged ethnic Russians to move in. The Soviets also built huge irrigation projects for more cotton production. In 1991 the Soviet government collapsed. Central Asia's republics became independent countries.

> **What happened to Central Asia's republics when the Soviet government collapsed in 1991?**
>
> _____
> _____

CULTURE

The people who came through Central Asia brought new languages, religions, and ways of life. These mixed with traditional ways.

For centuries, Central Asians raised horses, cattle, goats, and sheep. Many lived as **nomads.** They moved their herds to different pastures in summer and winter. They also moved their houses. The Central Asian nomad's moveable house is called a **yurt.** It is an important symbol today, even though most people now live in permanent settlements. Even people in cities put up yurts for special events. Nomads, though, are still common in Kyrgyzstan.

Today, most of the region's ethnic groups are part of the larger Turkic group. There are ethnic Russians, also. Each group speaks its own language. Most countries have more than one official language. In some, Russian is still the

Guided Reading Workbook

official language because of earlier Russian rule. The Russians also brought Cyrillic, their alphabet. Now most countries use the Latin alphabet, the one for writing English. However, Afghanistan uses its own alphabet for writing Pashto, one of its official languages.

The region's main religion is Islam, but there are also others. Some people are Russian Orthodox, a Christian religion. Today, many religious buildings that were closed by the Soviets have opened again.

| Why do many people in Central Asian countries speak Russian? |
| _____ |
| _____ |

CENTRAL ASIA TODAY

Central Asia is working to recover from a history of invasions and foreign rulers. The region is trying to build more stable governments and stronger economies.

In the 1980s Afghanistan fought a war with the Soviet Union that ended in 1989. It left the country in turmoil. In the mid-1990s, the **Taliban** took power. This was a radical Muslim group. It ruled most of the country, including **Kabul,** the capital. It based its laws on strict Islamic teachings. Women's lives were very limited, and even music and dancing were banned. Most people disagreed with the Taliban, but it stayed in power for many years.

| What group ruled Afghanistan from the mid-1990s to 2001? |
| _____ |

On September 11, 2001, a terrorist group called al Qaeda attacked the United States. The group was based in Afghanistan and linked to the Taliban. As a result, U.S. and British forces attacked and toppled the Taliban government. Now people in Afghanistan have a constitution and can vote. Women have more freedom. However, the Taliban is trying to regain power and continues to cause problems.

Kazakhstan was the first part of Central Asia that Russia conquered. It still has many Russian influences. About one third of its people are ethnic Russian and many people speak both

| Describe three changes that have happened in Afghanistan since the fall of the Taliban. |
| _____ |
| _____ |
| _____ |

Russian and Kazakh. Kazakhstan's economy
suffered when the Soviet Union fell. But it is
growing again because of oil reserves and a free
market. The country is the richest in Central
Asia. Kazakhstan also has a stable democratic
government. People elect a president and
parliament.

In Kyrgyzstan, clan membership is an
important part of social, political, and economic
life. Many people still follow nomadic traditions,
though there are also many that farm. Farmers
use both irrigation and **dryland farming,** which
relies on rainfall. Farming is the most important
industry in Kyrgyzstan, but it does not provide
much income for the country. Tourism is helping
to strengthen the economy. The government is
also changing. In 2010, the president was
overthrown. A new constitution was adopted and
first-ever elections were held.

> Circle the name of the
> industry that is
> strengthening Kyrgyzstan's
> economy.

Tajikistan has many problems. In the 1990s
rebels fought the Communist government. Some
wanted democracy and some wanted Islamic law.
In 1997 the groups ended the conflict. Now
Tajikistan is a republic with an elected president.
Years of war ruined the country's economy. Today,
the economy relies on cotton farming. But
progress is difficult because only about 7 percent
of the land is **arable,** or suitable for growing crops.

> Why should Tajikistan look
> for other ways to support
> its economy?
> _____
> _____

Turkmenistan's president is elected for life by
the country's parliament. He has all the power.
He has made education, health, and technology
reforms. The government supports Islamic
principles, but tries to keep them separate from
politics. Turkmenistan's economy is based on oil,
gas, and cotton. About half the country is
planted with cotton, even though it is a desert.
This is possible because Turkmenistan has one of
the longest irrigation channels in the world.

> Why does Turkmenistan
> have such a long irrigation
> channel?
> _____
> _____

Uzbekistan has the largest population and
cities in Central Asia. The United States criticizes

the government because it restricts political freedom and human rights. Its elected president holds all the power. The government also controls the economy, which is based on oil, gold, and cotton. The economy is stable, but is growing very slowly.

ISSUES AND CHALLENGES

Central Asia faces challenges in three areas today: environment, economy, and politics.

The shrinking Aral Sea is a serious problem for Central Asia's environment. The seafloor is dry. Dust, salt, and pesticides blow out of it. Towns that relied on fishing are now miles from shore. Another problem is leftover radiation from Soviet nuclear testing. It causes people's health to suffer. Crop chemicals are also a threat. They have been used too much and ended up ruining farmlands.

> Underline the main environmental challenges that Central Asian countries face.

Central Asia's economy relies on only one crop—cotton. Since there is little farmland, there are limited jobs. Oil and gas reserves may bring in more money one day. However, old equipment, lack of funds, and poor transportation slow development.

Central Asia does not have widespread political stability. In some countries, like Kyrgyszstan, people do not agree on the best kind of government. Often, these people turn to violence or terrorism, which threaten their own countries.

CHALLENGE ACTIVITY

Critical Thinking: Analyze Information If you were asked to plan a meeting about protecting the environment in Central Asia, what topics would you put on the agenda? What topic would you want to spend the most time discussing?

The Eastern Mediterranean

MAIN IDEAS
1. Turkey's history includes invasion by the Romans, rule by the Ottomans, and a 20th-century democracy.
2. Turkey's people are mostly ethnic Turks, and its culture is a mixture of modern and traditional.
3. Today, Turkey is a democratic nation seeking economic opportunities and considering European Union membership.

Key Terms and Places

Istanbul Turkey's largest city

janissaries slave boys converted to Islam and trained as soldiers

Ankara capital of Turkey

secular religion is kept separate from government

Lesson Summary
HISTORY

About 8,000 years ago, the area that is now Turkey was home to the world's earliest farming villages. The region was invaded for centuries. The ancient Greeks created the city of Byzantium, which is now the site of modern **Istanbul.** Romans captured Byzantium and changed the name to Constantinople. The city was an important trading port because it was at the crossroads between Europe and Asia. After the fall of Rome, Constantinople became the capital of the Byzantine Empire.

Seljuk Turks, a nomadic people from Central Asia, invaded the area in the AD 1000s. In the mid-1200s, Muslim Turkish warriors, known as the Ottomans, took territory from the Christian Byzantine Empire. The Ottomans had an army with fiercely loyal soldiers. Many of these were **janissaries,** Christian boys from conquered areas who converted to Islam. The army also had new weapons, including gunpowder.

> **What did the Romans rename Byzantium?**
> _____

> **Who were the Seljuk Turks?**
> _____
> _____
> _____
> _____

Lesson 2, *continued*

In 1453 the Ottoman Turks, led by Mehmed II "the Conqueror," captured Constantinople and defeated the Byzantine Empire. He changed the name of Constantinople to Istanbul and made it his capital. He also turned the great church Hagia Sophia into a mosque.

After Mehmed's death, other rulers, or sultans, continued to expand the empire. They conquered Asia Minor, Syria, Egypt, and the holy cities of Mecca and Medina. The Ottoman Empire reached its height under Suleyman I "the Magnificent." From 1520 to 1566, the Ottomans took control of the eastern Mediterranean and pushed into Europe.

> **Circle the names of two Ottoman rulers who greatly expanded the empire.**

The Ottoman Empire stayed powerful during the 1500s and 1600s. It controlled territory in northern Africa, southwestern Asia, and southeastern Europe through the 1800s. In the early 1900s, the Ottomans fought on the losing side of World War I. They lost most of their territory at the end of the war.

Military officers, led by Mustafa Kemal, took over the government after World War I. Mustafa Kemal later adopted the name Kemal Atatürk, which means Father of Turks. Atatürk created the democratic nation of Turkey and moved the capital to **Ankara** from Constantinople, which he officially renamed Istanbul.

> **Who was the leader of Turkey after World War I?**
> _____

Atatürk wanted to modernize Turkey to make it stronger. He adopted some elements of western culture. He also banned the wearing of certain traditional Turkish clothing like veils and the fez. Women were encouraged to vote, work, and hold office. He also replaced the Arabic alphabet with the Latin alphabet, and adopted the metric system.

> **Why did Atatürk make so many changes and laws?**
> _____
> _____
> _____
> _____

The Eastern Mediterranean

MAIN IDEAS
1. Israel's history includes the ancient Israelites and the creation of the State of Israel.
2. In Israel today, Jewish culture is a major part of daily life.
3. The Palestinian Territories are areas next to Israel—Gaza and the West Bank—controlled partly by Palestinian Arabs.

Key Terms and Places

Judaism religion of the Jewish people and the oldest monotheistic religion

Diaspora scattering of the Jewish population

Jerusalem capital of Israel

Zionism movement that called for Jews to reestablish a Jewish state in Palestine

kosher term used for food allowed under Jewish dietary laws

kibbutz large farm where people share everything in common

Gaza small, crowded piece of coastal land disputed over by Jews and Arabs

West Bank largely populated, rural piece of land disputed over by Jews and Arabs

Lesson Summary
HISTORY

Israel is often referred to as the Holy Land. It is home to sacred sites for three major religions: **Judaism,** Christianity, and Islam. Many events in the Jewish and Christian Bibles happened in Israel.

The Israelites established the kingdom of Israel about 1000 BC. In the 60s BC, the Romans conquered the region. They renamed it Palestine in AD 135. After several Jewish revolts, the Romans forced many Jews to leave the region and move to other lands. This was known as the **Diaspora.**

Arabs conquered Palestine in the mid-600s, but during the Crusades, it was invaded by Christians. The Crusaders captured the city of **Jerusalem** in 1099 but were eventually driven out.

> **Why is Israel often referred to as the Holy Land?**
> _____
> _____
> _____
> _____

> **When did Arabs conquer Palestine?**
> _____

Lesson 3, *continued*

Palestine was part of the Ottoman Empire until it came under British control after World War I.

In the late 1800s, European Jews began a movement called **Zionism.** It called for Jews to reestablish a Jewish state in their ancient homeland. Many thousands of Jews and Arabs moved to the region, then under British control. Arabs also moved there to counterbalance the number of Jews moving into the region. In 1947 the United Nations voted to divide the Palestine Mandate into Jewish and Arab states. Arab countries rejected this plan. The Jews accepted it and a year later created the State of Israel. Five Arab armies invaded Israel but were defeated. Many Palestinians then fled to neighboring Arab countries. Israel and Arab countries have fought several wars since, and disputes between the two sides continue today.

> **What is Zionism?**
> _____
> _____
> _____
> _____

ISRAEL TODAY

Jews from all over the world have come to Israel, hoping to find peace and stability. Yet the country faces continual conflicts with neighboring countries. Despite this, Israel is a modern, democratic country. It has a prime minister and parliament. The country also has a strong military, in which most men and women serve for at least one year.

> **Why does Israel have such a strong military?**
> _____
> _____
> _____

Israel has a modern, diverse economy. It exports high-tech equipment and cut diamonds. Irrigation increases food production. Millions of visitors come to see the historic sites.

Most Israelis live in cities. Jerusalem, the capital, and Tel Aviv are Israel's largest cities. About 75 percent of Israel's population is Jewish. The rest of the population is mostly Arab. While most Arabs are Muslim, about a quarter are Christian. Both Hebrew and Arabic are official languages.

> **What percentage of Israel's population is Jewish?**
> _____

The Eastern Mediterranean

MAIN IDEAS
1. Syria is an Arab country that has been ruled by a powerful family and recently torn by civil war.
2. Lebanon is recovering from civil war, and its people are divided by religion.
3. Jordan has few resources and is home to Bedouins and Palestinian refugees.

Key Terms and Places

Damascus capital of Syria

Beirut capital of Lebanon

Bedouins Arab-speaking nomads who mostly live in the deserts of Southwest Asia

Amman capital of Jordan

Lesson Summary
SYRIA

Syria, Lebanon, and Jordan all border Israel and have had conflicts with it. They have majority Arab populations and share a similar history, religion, and culture.

The capital of Syria, **Damascus,** is believed to be the oldest continuously inhabited city in the world. Syria became part of the Ottoman Empire in the 1500s. After World War I, France controlled Syria. Syria gained independence in the 1940s.

From 1971 to 2000, Syria was ruled by the dictator Hafiz al-Assad. He increased Syria's military to protect himself from political enemies and to match Israel's military strength. Assad's son, Bashar, was elected president after his father's death in 2000. In 2011 anti-government protesters challenged Bashar al-Assad's rule. Syria used brutal force to crush the protests. By 2012 Syria was divided by a civil war.

About 23 million people live in Syria. Almost 90 percent of the population is Arab. The remaining 10 percent include Kurds and Armenians.

> Which country controlled Syria after World War I?
> _____

> What caused the civil war in Syria?
> _____
> _____
> _____
> _____
> _____
> _____

About 74 percent of Syria's Muslims are Sunni, and the rest are smaller Islamic groups. Syria also has Christians and some small Jewish communities.

The civil war has drastically affected the population. By March 2017 over 386,000 Syrian people had died as a result of the fighting. More than 11 million have lost their homes, and almost 5 million refugees have left the country.

LEBANON

Lebanon is a small, mountainous country on the Mediterranean coast. Many ethnic minority groups settled in Lebanon during the Ottoman Empire. After World War I, it was controlled by France. Lebanon finally gained its independence in the 1940s.

> **When did Lebanon gain its independence?**
> _____

Most Lebanese people are Arab, but they are divided by religion. The main religions in Lebanon are Islam and Christianity. Both religions are divided into smaller groups. Muslims are divided into Sunni and Shia. Islam is Lebanon's majority religion.

> **What are the two main religious groups in Lebanon?**
> _____

After independence, Christians and Muslims shared political power. However, over time tensions mounted and civil war broke out. In the 1970s Muslims fought against Christians. Other countries, including Syria and Israel, got involved. Many people died and the capital, **Beirut,** was badly damaged.

> **When did Lebanon's civil war take place?**
> _____
> _____

Warfare lasted until 1990. After that, Syrian troops stayed in Lebanon. They were pressured to leave in 2005. However, border attacks from Lebanon against Israel led to fighting between those two countries.

JORDAN

The country of Jordan was created after World War I. Britain controlled the area until the 1940s, when the country gained full independence.

North Africa

MAIN IDEAS

1. Major physical features of North Africa include the Nile River, the Sahara, and the Atlas Mountains.
2. The climate of North Africa is hot and dry, and water is the region's most important resource.

Key Terms and Places

Sahara world's largest desert, covering most of North Africa

Nile River world's longest river, located in Egypt

silt finely ground fertile soil good for growing crops

Suez Canal strategic waterway connecting the Mediterranean and Red Seas

oasis wet, fertile area in a desert where a natural spring or well provides water

Atlas Mountains mountain range on the northwestern side of the Sahara

Lesson Summary
PHYSICAL FEATURES

Morocco, Algeria, Tunisia, Libya, and Egypt are the five countries of North Africa. All five countries have northern coastlines on the Mediterranean Sea. The largest desert in the world, the **Sahara,** covers most of North Africa.

The **Nile River,** the world's longest river, flows northward through the eastern Sahara. Near its end, the Nile becomes a large river delta that empties into the Mediterranean Sea. The river's water irrigates the farmland along its banks. In the past, flooding along the Nile left finely ground fertile soil, called **silt,** in the surrounding fields. Today, the Aswan High Dam controls flooding and prevents silt from being deposited in the nearby fields. Farmers must use fertilizer to aid the growth of crops.

East of the Nile River is the Sinai Peninsula, which is made up of rocky mountains and desert.

Name the five countries of North Africa.
_____
_____

Describe the Nile River.
_____
_____
_____
_____
_____
_____

The **Suez Canal,** a narrow waterway, connects the Mediterranean Sea with the Red Sea. Today large cargo ships carry oil and other goods through the canal.

The Sahara has a huge impact on all North Africa. It is made up of sand dunes, gravel plains, and rocky, barren mountains. Because of the Sahara's harsh environment, few people live there. Small settlements of farmers are located by **oases**—wet, fertile areas in the desert that are fed by natural springs. Oases provide a shady place to rest in the desert. The Ahaggar Mountains are located in central North Africa. The **Atlas Mountains** are in the northwestern part of North Africa.

> Why would an oasis be valuable to someone traveling in the desert?
>
> _____
> _____
> _____

CLIMATE AND RESOURCES

Most of North Africa has a desert climate. It is hot and dry during the day and cool or cold during the night. There is very little rain. Most of the northern coast west of Egypt has a Mediterranean climate. There it is hot and dry in the summer and cool and moist in the winter. Areas between the coast and the Sahara have a steppe climate.

> What kind of climate covers most of North Africa?
>
> _____

Important resources include oil and gas, particularly for Libya, Algeria, and Egypt. In Morocco, iron ore and minerals are important. Coal, oil, and natural gas are found in the Sahara.

CHALLENGE ACTIVITY

Critical Thinking: Evaluate Why do you think almost all of Egypt's population lives along the Nile River? Write a brief paragraph that explains your answer.

rule, Egyptian cities such as **Cairo** became major centers of learning, trade, and craft making.

EGYPT TODAY

Egypt is North Africa's most populous country. More than 85 million people live there.

In 2011, a massive protest known as **Arab Spring** broke out. This wave of uprisings shook North Africa and Southwest Asia. Egypt's military forced President Hosni Mubarak from power, ending 30 years of autocratic rule. Since an autocratic ruler has absolute power, people living under this type of regime do not have the power to vote or express their true thoughts on the government.

Egyptians elected Mohamed Morsi in 2012. Morsi had the support of the Muslim Brotherhood, a group that believes all aspects of society should be based on Islamic law. However, the Egyptian people were still divided and unhappy. This resulted in a massive protest for Morsi's resignation. In May 2014, former general Abdel Fattah el-Sisi was elected president.

Egypt is challenged by its limited resources. The only farmland is along the Nile River. Farmers use fertilizers to make the land productive. Still, Egypt must import much of its food.

The Suez Canal is an important part of Egypt's economy. It makes more than $5 billion a year in tolls. It is one of the world's busiest waterways.

Ninety-nine percent of Egyptians live in the Nile valley and delta. Cairo, Egypt's capital and largest city, is located in this Nile valley. Cairo's location at the southern end of the Nile delta helped the city grow to around 18 million people. Today Cairo is a mixture of modern buildings, historic mosques, and mud-brick houses.

Except for Cairo and Alexandria, Egypt's second-largest city, more than half of all

> **How many Egyptians live in the Nile valley and delta?**
>
> _____

Egyptians live in small villages and other rural areas. Farmers own very small plots of land along the Nile River.

CULTURES

Egypt shares much of its history and culture with other countries of North Africa. Egyptians, Berbers, and Bedouins make up almost all of Egypt's population. Most Egyptians and North Africans speak Arabic. About 90 percent of Egyptians are Muslims who practice the religion of Islam.

> **What religion do most Egyptians practice?**
> _____

Grains, vegetables, fruits, and nuts are common foods. Couscous, a pellet-like pasta made from wheat, is served steamed with vegetables or meat. Another favorite dish is *fuul*, made from fava beans. It is often served with hard-boiled eggs and bread.

Egypt observes two Revolution Day holidays. The one on January 25 celebrates the 2011 revolution, while the one on January 23 celebrates the 1962 revolution, when Egypt gained its independence from Britain.

There are two important religious holidays that Egyptians observe as well. The birthday of Muhammad, the prophet of Islam, is marked with lights, parades, and special sweets. Ramadan is a holy month during which Muslims fast.

North Africa is known for its beautiful architecture, wood carving, carpets, and hand-painted tiles. Egypt has produced important writers, including Egypt's Nobel Prize winner Naguib Mahfouz. Egypt also has a thriving film industry.

CHALLENGE ACTIVITY

Critical Thinking: Elaborate Imagine that you are traveling throughout Egypt. Write a letter to a friend at home that describes the people you meet and the places you visit.

and Tunisia each won independence. Algeria did not win independence until 1962.

Most people in North Africa are of mixed Arab and Berber ancestry. The majority of North Africans speak Arabic, but some also speak French, Italian, and English.

Since most North Africans are Muslim, they observe holidays such as Muhammad's birthday and the holy month of Ramadan. Men like to gather in cafes where they can play chess or dominoes. Most North African women socialize only in their homes.

> Underline the sentence that lists the holidays often observed in North Africa.

North Africa is famous for beautiful hand-woven carpets. These carpets are woven with bright colors and complex geometric patterns. Detailed hand-painted tilework is also a major art form in the region. North Africans also enjoy popular music based on singing and poetry. The musical scale there has many more notes than are common in Western music, which makes the tunes seem to wail or waver.

COUNTRIES OF NORTH AFRICA

Western Libya, Tunisia, Algeria, and Morocco are known as the **Maghreb.** The Sahara covers most of this region. Oil is the most important resource, and agriculture is a major economic activity. Tourism is also important, especially in Tunisia and Morocco. Marketplaces called **souks** jam the narrow streets of many North African cities, such as the Casbah in Algiers, the capital of Algeria. There they sell spices, carpets, copper teapots, and other goods. Tangier, in Morocco, overlooks the Strait of Gibraltar to Spain and is a **free port.** Almost no taxes are charged on goods sold there.

The countries of North Africa share similar economies and challenges. Until 2011 Muammar Gaddafi was Libya's dictator. His crackdown on protesters led to a civil war in which his regime

> Who was Libya's dictator until 2011?
>
> _____

toppled. The country's economy suffered after the civil war, but OPEC allowed Libya to increase oil production. The country's economy seems to be back on its way to recovery.

After a series of protests in 2011, Algeria's government has made reforms. It eased restrictions on the media, political parties, and the ability of women to serve in elected office. Since forcing longtime President Zine al-Abidine Ben Ali from power, Tunisia has held democratic elections and struggled with the role of Islam in government and society. Morocco is the only North African country with little oil, but it is an important producer and exporter of fertilizer.

CHALLENGE ACTIVITY

Critical Thinking: Categorize Create a chart that lists four cities in North Africa, and include facts about each one.

or "upright man," may have appeared in Africa about 1.5 million years ago. Scientists think these people walked completely upright and knew how to control fire. They used it to cook food, for heat, and as protection against wild animals. Modern humans are called *Homo sapiens*, or "wise man." Another Australopithecus was found in Ethiopia in 1974 by Donald Johanson. He named his find Lucy. In 1976, Mary Leakey found fossilized hominid footprints in Tanzania. Most of these finds were in East Africa, but hominid remains have been found in other parts of Africa. These discoveries have helped scholars trace the spread of early people across Africa.

> **How was Lucy similar to Mary Leakey's 1959 find?**
> _____
> _____
> _____

THE STONE AND IRON AGES

The Stone Age lasted more than 2.5 million years in some places. To make this long period of time easier to understand, scientists have divided it into three periods. In the Early Stone Age, people learned to shape stone into tools. They used these tools for tasks such as digging up roots and hunting small animals. The tools became more complex as time went by. The hand ax, usually made of flint, was shaped into a rough oval. One side of the oval was sharpened for cutting. The other side was rounded, making it easier to hold. Early Stone Age people were **hunter-gatherers** who lived in caves for protection from weather and animals. At times, they decorated these caves with scenes of hunting or other activities. This **rock art** can be found throughout Africa.

> **Why was the hand ax easier to use than the first stone tools?**
> _____
> _____
> _____
> _____

The Middle Stone Age began at different times in different parts of Africa. Tools made in the Middle Stone Age were smaller and had sharper edges. People attached handles of bone or wood to these tools to make spears, axes, and other useful tools. New tools helped people adapt to new environments and settle in other parts of Africa.

In the Later Stone Age, people made advanced tools, including knives and saws. They also used the bow and arrow for hunting. They wove baskets and made pottery containers for cooking and storage. People all over Africa learned to plant crops and herd animals. This provided a steady supply of food and allowed people to settle in permanent communities. People in these communities developed distinct lifestyles.

The Stone Age ended when people learned how to make tools out of metal. Iron was the most common metal used to make tools in Africa. Iron tools are very strong and sharp. Evidence shows that Africans had begun making iron tools in some places by about 600 BC.

> Underline the sentence that describes iron tools.

AFRICANS ADAPT TO DIFFERENT ENVIRONMENTS

As people settled various parts of Africa during the Stone Age, they developed distinct cultures. These cultures were influenced by the surrounding environment. Some African cultures remained in the Stone Age until modern times. Anthropologists have studied the traditional ways of these modern Stone Age cultures, and this has helped them understand how people lived thousands of years ago. The Bambuti people live in the tropical rain forests of the Congo Basin. They are **nomads** who use bows, arrows, and spears to hunt animals. They gather wild yams, fruits, berries, and other plants. The San people of the Kalahari Desert are also hunter-gatherers. They use tools of wood, bone, reeds, and stone. They hunt with snares, by throwing sticks, and with bows and arrows. They have learned to adapt to their dry environment. The Maasai people in the savanna of East Africa have also adapted to their environment. They herd cattle and other animals instead of hunting and gathering. They are known as fierce warriors.

> Circle the names of three Stone Age cultures. Underline the words that describe their environments.

Empire. However, in the 600s and 700s, Muslim armies from Southwest Asia conquered most of North Africa. Though Aksum itself was never conquered, it became isolated from other lands. The descendants of the Aksum people formed a new kingdom called Ethiopia. By about 1150, Ethiopia had become a powerful kingdom. Like Aksum, Ethiopia was a Christian kingdom. Shared beliefs helped unify Ethiopians, but their isolation from other Christians led to changes in their beliefs. Some local African customs blended with Christian teachings. This resulted in a new form of Christianity called **Coptic Christianity.** Most Christians who live in North Africa today belong to Coptic churches.

When did Ethiopia become a powerful kingdom?
_____
_____

GHANA CONTROLS TRADE

Ghana's territory lay between the Sahara Desert to the north and deep forests to the south. Salt was found in the Sahara, and gold was mined in the south. Ghana was in a good position to control trade in these items. This trade often followed the process of **silent barter.** This ensured peaceful trading and kept the location of the gold mines secret from the salt traders. The power of Ghana and its rulers grew as trade increased.

What made Ghana powerful?
_____
_____

By 800 Ghana controlled West Africa's trade routes. Ghana's army protected traders. Traders paid taxes on goods they brought into Ghana and goods they took out. The people of Ghana also paid taxes. The kings conquered more territory and became rich. The empire of Ghana reached its peak under the ruler Tunka Manin.

By the end of the 1200s, Ghana had collapsed. Three major factors contributed to its decline. First, a Muslim group called the Almoravids invaded and weakened the empire. Second, the Almoravids brought herds of animals that overgrazed pastures. This ruined the farmland and caused many farmers to leave. The third

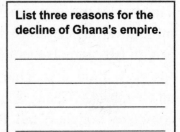

List three reasons for the decline of Ghana's empire.

_____

_____

_____

_____

factor was a rebellion by people Ghana had conquered.

MALI BUILDS ON GHANA'S FOUNDATION

Once Ghana's empire fell, Mali took control of the trade routes. Mali became powerful under a ruler named Sundiata (soohn-JAHT-ah). He freed Mali from a cruel ruler. Then he conquered nearby kingdoms, including Ghana, and took over the salt and gold trades and the religious and political authority. Mali reached its peak under a Muslim named Mansa Musa. Musa ruled Mali for about 25 years and captured many important trading cities, including **Timbuktu.** On his pilgrimage to Mecca, he brought attention to Islam throughout West Africa by building **mosques.** After Mansa Musa died, invaders destroyed the schools and mosques of Timbuktu. By 1500 nearly all the lands of the Mali empire were lost.

> Name two important things Mansa Musa did as leader of Mali.
>
> _____
> _____
> _____
> _____

SONGHAI TAKES OVER

As the empire of Mali reached its height, the Songhai (SAHNG-hy) kingdom was growing strong. From their capital at **Gao,** the Songhai participated in the same trade that had made Ghana and Mali rich. When Mali control weakened, the Songhai broke free. Songhai leader Sunni Ali strengthened and enlarged the Songhai empire. Songhai reached its peak under a ruler named Askia the Great. Muslim culture and education blossomed during Askia's reign. Timbuktu's universities, schools, libraries, and mosques attracted thousands of people. **Djenné** was an important center of learning. In 1591, Morocco invaded Songhai and destroyed Gao and Timbuktu. Changes in trade patterns completed Songhai's fall. Port cities became more important and replaced trading over land routes.

> Circle the names of two cities that were important centers of learning in the Songhai empire.

History of Sub-Saharan Africa

MAIN IDEAS
1. Trade led to the spread of Islam in East Africa.
2. Europeans arrived in Africa in search of valuable trade goods.
3. The slave trade had terrible effects in Africa.
4. Many European countries established colonies in Africa.

Key Terms and Places

Swahili language and culture created from blending African and Arab influences

Middle Passage brutal trip to take slaves across the Atlantic

Gold Coast first European colony in West Africa

Lesson Summary
TRADE IN EAST AFRICA

In the 1100s farmers and fishers lived in small villages along Africa's eastern coast. Their lives changed when traders from Asia traveled to Africa. Some traders were Muslims from India, Persia, and Arabia. They were looking for new kinds of goods they could sell at home. They also wanted Africans to buy goods from their homelands. African traders became rich by selling ivory, gold, and other items.

Growing trade caused coastal villages to become busy seaports. By 1300 they became major trading cities. Merchants from many countries brought manufactured goods, porcelain, and cotton. They traded their goods for East African cloth and iron. Muslim traders settled in many cities. Africans, Arabs, and Persians lived and worked together. As a result, Islam spread throughout East Africa.

The contact between cultures caused other changes in East Africa. For example, architecture changed. People combined traditional materials with Arabic designs for their houses. Language

> Circle the words that tell why coastal villages became busy seaports.

> List two things that changed because of the contact between cultures.
> _____
> _____

Lesson 3, *continued*

---

also changed. Africans who spoke Bantu adopted
Arabic and Persian words. The languages
combined to form **Swahili,** a new language.
Swahili also refers to the blended African-Arab
culture.

THE ARRIVAL OF EUROPEANS

In the late 1400s, many European explorers
searched for new trade routes to India and China.
The Portuguese sailed around Africa. Europeans
had heard rumors about gold in Africa. The
stories were about Mansa Musa, the ruler of
Mali. In the 1300s he traveled to Mecca. He gave
away gifts of gold as he traveled. The Portuguese
reached the coasts of West Africa. They learned
that the stories were true.

> Underline the sentence that tells what Europeans had heard about Africa.

Ivory was another valuable product in Africa.
Europeans used it for furniture, jewelry, statues,
and other items. The Portuguese traded mostly in
gold and ivory. Soon they found they could make
more money by selling slaves.

THE ATLANTIC SLAVE TRADE

Slavery had existed in Africa for centuries. Most
slaves had been captured in battle or from attacks
on enemies. The arrival of Europeans in West
Africa increased the demand for slaves.
Europeans wanted Africans to work as slaves on
their large farms in the Americas. They bought
the captured slaves and put them on ships. The
brutal trip to take slaves across the Atlantic was
called the **Middle Passage.** Slave traders made a
lot of money. Some Europeans argued against it,
but it continued for more than 300 years.
European governments finally stopped the slave
trade in the 1800s.

> When did the European governments stop the slave trade?
>
> _____
>
> _____

The slave trade had terrible effects in Africa. It
caused a sharp drop in Africa's population. Many
millions of Africans were taken to the Americas,
Europe, Asia, and the Middle East. The push to

> Underline the sentences that describe the slave trade's effects on Africa.

Guided Reading Workbook

MAIN IDEAS
1. The search for raw materials led to a new wave of European involvement in Africa.
2. The Scramble for Africa was a race by Europeans to form colonies there.
3. Some Africans resisted rule by Europeans.
4. Nationalism led to independence movements in Africa.

Key Terms and Places

entrepreneurs independent businesspeople

imperialism attempt to dominate a country's government, trade, or culture

ethnocentrism belief that your own group or culture is better or more important than others

Suez Canal waterway built in Egypt in the 1860s to connect the Mediterranean and Red Seas

Berlin Conference meeting of European leaders that led to the division of Africa among European powers

Boers Dutch farmers in South Africa

nationalism devotion or loyalty to a country

Lesson Summary
NEW INVOLVEMENT IN AFRICA

After the slave trade ended in the early 1800s, Europeans lost interest in Africa. However, factory owners needed raw materials. The huge open spaces and mineral wealth of Africa drew new colonists. Most were **entrepreneurs** who built mines, plantations, and trade routes with the dream of becoming rich. They often tried to dominate the government, trade, or culture of a country, a practice called **imperialism.** They believed that their own government and culture were better than native African ways. Because of this European **ethnocentrism,** Africans were forced to adopt many elements of European culture.

> What did entrepreneurs hope to gain in Africa?
> _____
> _____

European governments also became involved in Africa. This was often an extension of national rivalries. Each country wanted to control more land and more colonies than its rivals did. The English government got involved in Africa to protect British investments in the **Suez Canal.** Egypt's government was unstable in the 1880s. This made the British fear they would lose access to the canal. The British moved into Egypt and took partial control of the country to protect their shipping routes. In South Africa, diamonds were discovered. The De Beers Consolidated Mine Company, owned by Englishman Cecil Rhodes, came to control the diamond market.

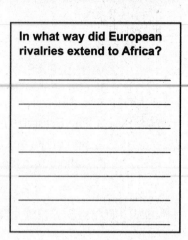

In what way did European rivalries extend to Africa?

_____
_____
_____
_____
_____
_____

THE SCRAMBLE FOR AFRICA

European countries rushed to claim as much land in Africa as they could. Conflicts arose as countries tried to claim the same area. To prevent these conflicts from developing into wars, Europe's leaders met in the **Berlin Conference** to divide up Africa. The boundaries they drew for their colonies often divided kingdoms, clans, and families. In time, the Europeans' disregard for Africans led to problems for Europeans and Africans alike. In South Africa, war broke out between British and Dutch settlers. The **Boers** had been in South Africa since the late 1600s. In 1899, the British tried to make the Boers' land part of the British Empire. The Boers fought a guerrilla war, but the British dealt harshly with them. South Africa became a British colony.

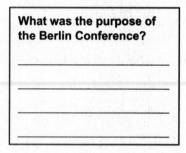

What was the purpose of the Berlin Conference?

_____
_____
_____

AFRICAN RESISTANCE

The African people fought against rule by Europeans and against adopting European ways. Especially strong resistance came from the Zulu of South Africa and the Ethiopians. A Zulu leader named Shaka brought together various tribes to form a single nation. This nation was so

How did Shaka make the Zulu people especially strong?

_____
_____
_____
_____

West and Central Africa

MAIN IDEAS

1. West Africa's key physical features include plains and the Niger River.
2. West Africa has distinct climate and vegetation zones, such as arid and tropical.
3. Central Africa's major physical features include the Congo Basin and plateaus surrounding the basin.
4. Central Africa has a humid tropical climate and dense forest vegetation.

Key Terms and Places

Niger River most important river in West Africa

zonal organized by zone

Sahel strip of land that divides the desert from wetter areas

desertification spread of desert-like conditions

savanna area of tall grasses and scattered trees and shrubs

Congo Basin basin near the middle of Central Africa

basin generally flat region surrounded by higher land such as mountains and plateaus

Congo River river that drains the Congo Basin and empties into the Atlantic Ocean

Zambezi River river that flows eastward toward the Indian Ocean

Lesson Summary

PHYSICAL FEATURES OF WEST AFRICA

The main physical features in West Africa are plains and rivers. Most of the region's cities are on the plains along the coast. People on inland plains usually farm or raise animals. The **Niger River** is the most important river in the region. It provides water for farming, fishing, and transportation.

> Underline the sentence that describes the importance of the Niger River to the region.

CLIMATE AND VEGETATION

West Africa has four **zonal** climate regions that run in east to west bands. The zone farthest north is part of the largest desert in the world, the Sahara. The **Sahel,** south of the Sahara, has a steppe climate where enough plants grow to support some grazing animals. Overgrazing and cutting trees for firewood have caused **desertification.** The third zonal area, the **savanna,** is a good area for farming. The coastal areas have a humid tropical climate with tropical forests. The climate of the savanna is milder than other parts of Africa. The fourth climate zone lies along the coasts of the Atlantic and the Gulf of Guinea. This zone has a humid tropical climate with plentiful rainfall.

What are two causes of desertification?
_____
_____

PHYSICAL FEATURES OF CENTRAL AFRICA

The **Congo Basin** lies near the middle of the region. Plateaus and low hills surround the **basin.** A basin is shaped like a big soup bowl with a wide brim. The highest mountains in Central Africa lie east along the Western Rift Valley. The **Congo River** drains the Congo Basin and has hundreds of smaller rivers flowing into it. The many rapids and waterfalls prevent ships sailing from the interior to the Atlantic. Many rivers join the **Zambezi River** before it reaches the Indian Ocean. Victoria Falls is the most famous falls on the Zambezi River.

Where are the tallest mountains in the region found?
_____
_____
_____

CLIMATE, VEGETATION, AND ANIMALS

The Congo Basin and much of the Atlantic coast have a humid tropical climate. The dense tropical forests that grow in this climate are home to gorillas, elephants, wild boars, and okapis. Since little sunlight shines through the canopy, only a few animals live on the forest floor. Birds, monkeys, bats, and snakes live in the trees. Areas north and south of the Congo Basin have a tropical savanna climate. The mountains in the east have a highland climate. The southern part of the region has dry steppe and desert climates.

Name four animals that make their home in the tropical forests.
_____
_____
_____
_____

CULTURE

West Africa is the world's fastest growing region. Its culture reflects traditional African cultures, European culture, and Islam. There are hundreds of ethnic groups and languages in the region. Europeans drew the national boundaries without considering these ethnic groups or their rivalries, so many West Africans are more loyal to their ethnic group than to their country. Traditional religions are forms of **animism.** Islam and Christianity are also practiced. Some people in the region wear Western-style clothing. Others wear traditional cotton clothing, which is loose and flowing. Rural homes are made from mud or straw and have straw or tin roofs. **Extended families** often live close together in a village. An extended family includes the father, mother, children and close relatives in one household.

COASTAL COUNTRIES

Nigeria has the largest population in Africa and the region's strongest economy. There is conflict among the many different ethnic groups within Nigeria. After many years of military rule, Nigeria is now a democracy. Its most important resource is oil, which accounts for 95 percent of the country's export earnings. The main industrial center is **Lagos.** Nigeria has many resources but poverty is a problem. This is due partly to the high birthrate and corrupt government.

Small countries along the coast struggle to develop their economies and stabilize their governments. Senegal and Gambia produce peanuts and offer tourism sites. Guinea has some bauxite reserves. Guinea-Bissau has undeveloped mineral resources. Cape Verde is West Africa's only island country and has a democratic government. Liberia was founded for freed slaves. Both Liberia and Sierra Leone have suffered

> Circle three influences on West African societies.

> What are two causes of poverty in Nigeria?
> _____
> _____

> What two countries produce peanuts and offer tourism?
> _____
> _____

from violent civil war. They are now trying to rebuild. Ghana and Côte d'Ivoire have rich natural resources. Unstable governments and poor farming economies have hurt Togo and Benin.

SAHEL COUNTRIES

Drought and the expanding desert challenge the Sahel countries. Former nomads in Mauritania are now crowded into cities. Ethnic tensions continue to cause problems there. Niger has a very small amount of farmland where people grow staple crops. Drought and locusts created **famine** there in the early 2000s. Chad depends on fishing in Lake Chad and farming. Much of Lake Chad's water has evaporated in recent years, creating conflict over control of the remaining water. Chad began exporting oil in 2004. Much of Mali is desert with some farming in the south. It is one of the poorest countries in the world, but its economy is improving. Burkina Faso is also very poor and has few resources. Conflicts in the region have hurt its economy.

> Underline the causes of famine in Niger.

CHALLENGE ACTIVITY

Critical Thinking: Draw Inferences Write a letter to a newspaper to explain the problems that could arise from creating borders that put different ethnic groups in one country or separating ethnic groups into different countries.

independence, fighting continued among ethnic groups within the new countries. During the Cold War, the Soviet Union and the United States supported different groups in small wars that killed many people.

CULTURE

Many different languages and **dialects** are spoken in Central Africa. Most countries also have official European languages because of the influence of the European colonial powers. The colonial powers also brought Christianity to the region. Many Muslims live near the Sahel, and Muslims and Hindus live in Zambia.

The traditional cultures of Central Africa's ethnic groups have influenced the arts. The region is famous for sculpture, carved wooden masks, and colorful cotton gowns. The region is also the birthplace of a popular musical instrument called the *likembe*, or thumb piano, and a type of dance music called *makossa*.

What impact did colonial powers have on the culture of Central Africa?
_____
_____
_____
_____
_____
_____

RESOURCES AND COUNTRIES OF CENTRAL AFRICA

Most Central African countries are very poor. Because of colonial rule and civil wars, they have had problems building stable governments and strong economies.

Most people are subsistence farmers but are beginning to grow crops for sale. Common crops are coffee, bananas, and corn. In rural areas people sell goods at **periodic markets.** Rivers are important for travel, trade, and production of hydroelectricity. Timber, oil, natural gas, coal, copper, uranium, tin, zinc, diamonds, gold, and cobalt are found in the region. Most of Africa's copper is in the **copper belt.** However, political problems and poor transportation have kept these resources from being fully developed. Civil war, bad government, and crime have scared away foreign businesses.

Many people live in rural areas, but many are moving to the capital, **Kinshasa.** The city is crowded and has many slums. The Democratic Republic of the Congo was a Belgian colony until 1960. A military leader named Joseph Mobutu came to power in 1965 and ruled as a dictator. In 1997, after a civil war, a new government took over. The country has many mineral resources and is part of Centra Africa's rich copper belt.

Central African Republic has had military coups, corrupt leaders, and improper elections. Civil wars in the Republic of the Congo and Angola have hurt their governments and economies. Angola is troubled also by land mines left from its civil war, high **inflation,** and corrupt officials. The economies of many countries depend heavily on the sale of natural resources like oil, copper, and diamonds, or on export crops like coffee and cocoa. The Republic of the Congo has oil and forest products. Angola has diamonds and large oil deposits. Zambia's economy depends on copper mining. Malawi relies on farming and foreign aid. Oil discoveries in Equatorial Guinea and São Tomé and Príncipe may help their economies improve. Cameroon's stable government has helped its economy grow. It has good roads and railways. Gabon also has a stable government. Its economy is the strongest in the region. Half of its income comes from oil.

> Circle the issues that make progress difficult for Angola.

ISSUES AND CHALLENGES

The region faces serious challenges from wars, diseases such as **malaria** and AIDS, and threats to the environment. Deaths from wars and diseases have resulted in fewer older, more skilled workers. Other issues include food shortages and **malnutrition.** The region is also threatened by the destruction of tropical forests and the open-pit mining of diamonds and copper, which destroys the land.

> What diseases are creating challenges in Central Africa?
>
> _____
> _____

The East Africa Plateau is cut by rift valleys. East Africa has many volcanic mountains. The tallest of these is **Mount Kilimanjaro.** Although the mountain is located near the equator, its peak is covered with ice and snow. Another area of high elevation is the Ethiopian Highlands.

Grassy plains cover wide areas of the plateaus in East and Southern Africa. The **Serengeti Plain** in Tanzania is one of the largest. Many kinds of wildlife live here, including elephants, giraffes, lions, and zebras. Tanzania established much of the plain as a national park. The flat plains of Southern Africa are home to animals such as lions, leopards, elephants, baboons, and antelope.

The Nile, the world's longest river, begins in East Africa. It is formed by the White Nile and the Blue Nile. The White Nile flows from Lake Victoria. The Blue Nile begins in the Ethiopian Highlands. Both rivers meet in Sudan to form the Nile. Many large rivers cross Southern Africa's plains. The Okavango flows from Angola into a huge basin in Botswana. There, it forms a swampy inland delta that is home to crocodiles, zebras, hippos, and other animals. The Orange River passes through the Augrabies Falls and flows into the Atlantic Ocean.

CLIMATE AND VEGETATION

East Africa is cooler and dryer than other equatorial regions. This is because of the high elevations and the rain shadow effect that blocks wet weather from the region. The plateaus and mountains north of the equator have a cool highland climate and dense forests. A large savanna region extends south from the Equator and covers much of East and Southern Africa. In South Africa, these grasslands are known as the **veld.** The Kalahari Desert has grasses and shrubs in the north, but in the southwest it merges with

---

What is surprising about Mount Kilimanjaro?

_____

_____

_____

_____

Underline examples of wildlife that can be found on the Serengeti Plain.

Where is the veld located?

_____

the **Namib Desert.** Parts of the Namib Desert get as little as half an inch of rainfall in a year. Madagascar, off the mainland, has lush vegetation and tropical forests. It also has many animals that are found only in Madagascar. Unfortunately, rain forest destruction has endangered many of Madagascar's animals.

RESOURCES

Water is a vital resource in East and Southern Africa. Rivers supply hydroelectricity and water for irrigation. Where there is enough rain or where irrigation is possible, farmers can grow a wide range of crops. However, seasonal **droughts** are common. During a drought, crops and the grasses for cattle die, and people begin to starve. Important discoveries of gas and oil resources have been made in Mozambique, Tanzania, Uganda, and Kenya. Madagascar's forests provide timber. Most of the world's gold is mined in South Africa. Other mineral resources include diamonds, platinum, copper, uranium, coal, and iron ore. Mining is very important to Southern Africa's economy. However, mining can harm the surrounding natural environments.

What happens during a drought?
_____
_____
_____
_____

CHALLENGE ACTIVITY

Critical Thinking: Summarize Write a booklet for tourists to read before they embark on a helicopter tour of East and Southern Africa. What might they find most interesting about the region?

European nations increased their need for raw materials. European powers claimed lands and set up colonies, a process called **imperialism.** They competed in Africa to get natural resources such as gold, ivory, and rubber. The British controlled much of East Africa. The boundaries European leaders drew split ethnic groups apart and combined unfriendly groups. Most colonial rulers used African deputies to control the countries. Many deputies were traditional chiefs who often favored their own peoples. This caused conflict between ethnic groups. After 1945, nationalist movements formed throughout Africa. Most East African countries gained independence in the early 1960s.

> **Underline the sentence that explains the meaning of imperialism in Africa.**

CULTURE

East Africa's history has contributed to its great diversity of people and ways of life. As a result, East Africans speak many different languages and practice several religions. French is the official language in Rwanda, Burundi, and Djibouti. English is spoken in Uganda, Kenya, and Tanzania. Swahili is an African language spoken by about 80 million East Africans. The largest religious groups are Christian and Muslim, but many East Africans follow traditional animist religions. Some people combine animist worship with religions such as Christianity.

> **Circle the three main languages spoken in East Africa.**

EAST AFRICA TODAY

Tanzania and Kenya are popular tourist destinations. Tourists take **safaris** to see the wildlife. Much of Kenya has been set aside as national parkland to protect wildlife. Tanzania is rich in gold and diamonds, but most of its people are subsistence farmers. Coffee, flowers, and tea grow well in the rich volcanic soil of Kenya. **Geothermal energy** is another important resource.

> **Circle the crops grown in Kenya.**

Both nations have modern cities. Kenya's capital, Nairobi, is an industrial and railroad center. Tanzania's largest city, Dar es Salaam, is a business center with a busy port.

Sudan is a mix of Arab, Afro-Arab, and African cultures. Sudan's government has abused the human rights of ethnic and religious minorities. An Arab militia group has killed hundreds of thousands of people in a region of Sudan called **Darfur.** Uganda was a military dictatorship for several decades. It has been more democratic since 1986. About 80 percent of Ugandans work in agriculture. Coffee is the country's main export. Rwanda and Burundi have experienced conflict between ethnic groups, the Tutsi and Hutu. This conflict led to **genocide** in Rwanda in the 1990s, as the Hutu tried to completely wipe out the Tutsi.

> Underline the names of two ethnic groups in Rwanda and Burundi.

THE HORN OF AFRICA

Eritrea, Djibouti, Somalia, and Ethiopia make up the Horn of Africa. Eritrea was controlled by Italy, Great Britain, and Ethiopia. In 1992, after 32 years of armed conflict with Ethiopia, Eritrea gained independence. However, conflict and human rights abuses continue there. Djibouti is a small, desert country. It lies on an important shipping route, and its port is a major source of income. The Issa and the Afar people of Djibouti fought a civil war that ended in 2001.

> What four countries make up the Horn of Africa?
>
> _____
>
> _____
>
> _____
>
> _____

Somalia's deserts and dry savannas make poor farmland, but the economy still depends heavily on agriculture. Most Somalis are Muslim and share the same language and ethnic background. Still, the country is torn by chaos and violence, and there is no central government. Clans fight over grazing rights and control of port cities such as **Mogadishu.** Ethiopia is the only nation in the Horn of Africa that escaped European colonization. Ethiopia's mountains and

> Underline the descriptions of the land in Somalia and Ethiopia.

Guided Reading Workbook

interior. The British fought and defeated the Boers and the Zulu to control the Cape.

In 1910, South Africa gained independence from Great Britain. The struggle for independence in some other Southern African nations was long and violent. South Africa was ruled by whites. Black South Africans who opposed them formed the African National Congress (ANC). The white government set up a policy called **apartheid,** which separated whites and nonwhites. Blacks had to live in separate areas called **townships** and had few rights. The United States and other countries applied **sanctions** on South Africa. In the 1990s, South Africa ended its apartheid laws. ANC leader Nelson Mandela was elected president.

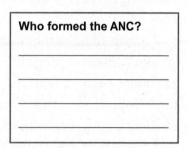

Who formed the ANC?

_____

_____

_____

_____

CULTURE

Southern Africa's people belong to hundreds of different ethnic groups. They speak many languages, most of which are related to Khoisan or Bantu. They practice different religions, including Christianity and traditional African religions. Southern Africa's arts reflect its many cultures, using traditional ethnic designs and crafts.

Most of Southern Africa's languages are related to what two languages?

_____

_____

SOUTHERN AFRICA TODAY

South Africa is a republic with an elected president. It has a strong economy with valuable mineral resources and industry. Johannesburg is Africa's largest industrial area. **Cape Town** attracts many tourists. Surrounded by South Africa, Lesotho and Swaziland are both **enclaves.** Both are also kingdoms, with a king and an elected prime minister and parliament. Namibia is a republic. Most of its income comes from mineral resources. Fishing and ranching are also important. Botswana is rich in mineral resources

What two things do Lesotho and Swaziland have in common?

_____

_____

_____

_____

and has a stable, democratic government. Cattle ranching and diamond mining are its main economic activities.

Zimbabwe has suffered from a poor economy, political instability, and inequality. In 2000, the president began a land reform program, taking land from white farmers and giving it to black residents. However, white farmers left the country and food shortages resulted. Mozambique is one of the world's poorest countries. The economy was damaged by a civil war. It relies on taxes collected on products from the interior of Africa that are shipped out of its ports. Madagascar has a struggling economy. The country is popular with tourists because of its unique plants and animals. Comoros is made up of four tiny islands. It is politically unstable and lacks resources. However, the government hopes to improve education and promote tourism.

> **What makes Madagascar a tourist destination?**
> _____
> _____

ISSUES AND CHALLENGES

Southern Africa faces many challenges, especially poverty, disease, and environmental destruction. The African Union (AU) is working to promote cooperation among African countries to try to solve these problems.

> **What is the AU and what is its purpose?**
> _____
> _____
> _____
> _____

CHALLENGE ACTIVITY

Critical Thinking: Contrast Contrast the economies and governments of Botswana and Zimbabwe. Write one or two sentences to explain how they are different from one another.

Lesson 1, *continued*

Harappa and Mohenjo-Daro. These cities were
well-planned and built in the shadow of a fortress
that could easily oversee the city streets. The
streets themselves were built at right angles and
had drainage systems. Buildings were made of
kiln-fired mud brick. These bricks were uniform
in size across Harappan civilization. The
Harappans also developed beautiful artisan
crafts, some of which have helped historians draw
conclusions about Harappan society.

A NEW CULTURE ARISES

The Aryan people may have arrived in India in
the 2000s BC. Historians do not know where they
came from, but over many centuries, they spread
into central India. They became the dominant
society in India during a time known as the Vedic
period or Vedic age. Much of what is known
about the Aryans comes from a collection of
religious writings called the Vedas. Unlike the
Harappans, Aryans lived in small communities
run by a local leader, or raja. Aryan groups
fought each other as often as they fought
outsiders. The Aryans spoke **Sanskrit** and
memorized poems and hymns that survived by
word of mouth. People later figured out how to
write Sanskrit. Today Sanskrit is the root of
many modern South Asian languages.

> How did the early Aryans preserve their poems and their history without writing?
>
> _____
> _____
> _____
> _____

VEDIC RELIGION AND EARLY HINDUISM

Religion was important during the Vedic age.
Many scholars call the early Hinduism of this
period Vedic religion or Brahmanism. This is
because of the religion's emphasis on the Vedas
and the belief in a divine reality known as
Brahman. The oldest of the Vedas is the Rigveda.
Over time, the Aryans wrote down their poems
and hymns in Sanskrit. These were compiled into
collections called Vedic texts. The texts described
rituals, such as how to perform sacrifices, and

> Underline the sentence that explains why early Hinduism is called Vedic religion or Brahmanism.

Guided Reading Workbook

offered reflections from religious scholars. By the
later Vedic period, powerful chiefs became rulers
over larger areas. Religious ceremonies provided
more power and status to these rulers, or kings.
The priests and upper class grew in importance
and wealth. This led to greater divisions in
ancient Indian society.

INDIAN SOCIETY DIVIDES

According to the Vedas, there were four main
varnas, or social divisions. The Brahmins were
priests. They were the highest-ranking varna. The
Kshatriyas were rulers or warriors. The Vaisyas
were commoners, including farmers, craftspeople,
and traders. The Sudras were workers and
servants. Another kind of division, called *jatis,*
was based on birth and had rules about how
these groups interacted with each other. The
varnas and the jatis developed into the **caste
system.** Castes were family based. A person's
caste determined his or her place in society, but at
first there was some social mobility among the
castes. Each caste had its own norms that people
in that caste followed. The Dalits, or
Untouchables, did not belong to any caste. In
ancient India, women had the same rights as
men, but over time, laws were passed to limit
these rights.

> **What are the four main
> *varnas,* or social divisions,
> in Indian society?**
>
> _____
> _____
> _____
> _____

Indian Early Civilizations, Empires, and World Religions

Lesson 3

MAIN IDEAS
1. Siddhartha Gautama searched for wisdom in many ways.
2. The teachings of Buddhism deal with finding peace.
3. Buddhism spread far from where it began in India.

Key Terms and Places

fasting going without food

meditation focusing of the mind on spiritual ideas

nirvana state of perfect peace

missionaries people who work to spread their religious beliefs

Lesson Summary
SIDDHARTHA'S SEARCH FOR WISDOM

In the late 500s BC, a major new religion began to develop from questions posed by a young prince named Siddhartha Gautama (si-DAHR-tuh GAU-tuh-muh). Siddhartha was born to a wealthy family and led a life of comfort, but he questioned the pain and suffering he saw all around him. Before the age of 30, Siddhartha left his home and family to look for answers about the meaning of life. He talked to many priests and wise men, but he was not satisfied with their answers.

Siddhartha did not give up. He wandered for years through the forests trying to free himself from daily concerns by **fasting** and **meditating.** After six years, Siddhartha sat down under a tree and meditated for seven weeks. He came up with an answer to what causes human suffering. Suffering is caused by wanting what one does not have, wanting to keep what one likes and already has, and not wanting what one dislikes but has. He began to travel and teach his ideas and was soon called the Buddha, or "Enlightened One."

> **Why did Siddhartha leave his life of luxury?**
>
> _____
> _____
> _____
> _____

> **What was Siddhartha called after he attained wisdom?**
>
> _____
> _____

TEACHINGS OF BUDDHISM

Buddhism is based upon the Four Noble Truths. These truths are as follows: suffering and unhappiness are part of life; suffering stems from our desire for pleasure and material goods; people can overcome their desires and reach **nirvana,** a state of perfect peace, which ends the cycle of reincarnation; and people can follow an eightfold path to nirvana, overcoming desire and ignorance.

These teachings were similar to some Hindu concepts, but went against some traditional Hindu ideas. Buddhism challenged the authority of the Brahmins. The Buddha said that each individual could reach salvation on his or her own. Buddhism also opposed the caste system.

What are the central teachings of Buddhism called?
_____
_____

What traditional Hindu ideas did Buddhism challenge?
_____
_____
_____

BUDDHISM SPREADS

Buddhism spread quickly throughout India. With the help of Indian king Asoka, Buddhist **missionaries** were sent to other countries to teach their religious beliefs. Missionaries introduced Buddhism to Sri Lanka and other parts of Southeast Asia, as well as Central Asia and Persia. It spread to China, Japan, and Korea. Eventually, Buddhism split into two major branches. Both branches have millions of believers today. Buddhists observe many holidays. Pilgrimage to holy sites is one of Buddhism's most important rituals.

Who sent missionaries to other countries?
_____
_____

CHALLENGE ACTIVITY

Critical Thinking: Compare Compare the roles of Constantine and Asoka in spreading Christianity and Buddhism. Write a paragraph to explain how they were alike.

access to God and is equal before God. They also
believe in the cycle of life, death, and
reincarnation, and in karma.

Sikh equality is seen in the **langar,** or kitchen,
of their places of worship. There, food is served
without charge and everyone sits together on the
floor to eat. This is a symbol of social equality.
Sikhs do observe the caste system in marriage
and in some **gurdwaras,** or places of worship.
Sikhs are expected to marry someone of their
own caste. Some castes have also created
gurdwaras for their caste only. A goal of Sikhism
is to become one with God. To do this, Sikhs
have three duties: to pray, to work, and to give.
This means keeping God in mind at all times.
God is kept in mind through prayer and
meditation, earning an honest living, and giving
to others. Sikhs also keep God in mind by
wearing special articles that signify their faith.
These articles include a turban, a sword, a metal
bracelet, and a wooden comb. In their quest for
spiritual liberation, Sikhs try to avoid five vices:
lust, greed, attachment to worldly things, anger,
and pride. Like other religions, Sikhs celebrate
special times for individuals and important
holidays for the community. An especially
important ceremony is Khalsa, when an adult
formally joins the Sikh community. Anniversaries
of events in the lives of the ten gurus are also
celebrated.

SIKH HISTORY

Many Sikhs lived in the Punjab region of India,
which was under the control of the Mughal
Empire. Sikhs were unfairly taxed and otherwise
mistreated. When they protested, the Mughal
Empire reacted harshly. Sikh resistance grew
stronger as the Mughal Empire weakened. In
1799, a man named Ranjit Singh declared
himself maharaja, or ruler of the Punjab. For the

> **What beliefs are shared by Sikhs and Hindus?**
> _____
> _____
> _____
> _____

> **Underline the three Sikh duties and circle the five vices.**

> **Who was Ranjit Singh?**
> _____
> _____
> _____
> _____

next 50 years, the Sikhs ruled much of what is now northwestern India and eastern Pakistan. During this time, a gurdwara in northwestern India was rebuilt using marble and gold as a symbol of Sikh power. It became known as the Golden Temple. Ranjit Singh was a strong ruler, and the Sikh Empire thrived during his life. However, when he died in 1839, the Sikh Empire began to weaken. The Punjab became a part of British India in 1849.

There are nearly 25 million Sikhs worldwide today. Most live in India. For many years, most migrant Sikhs were traders. After the British took control of India, Sikhs served as soldiers in British colonies in Malaya and Hong Kong. Sikhs began to migrate to other parts of the world. Living outside India has presented struggles and opportunities for Sikhs. There are now large Sikh communities in the United States and Canada. Their unique dress makes them very visible in their adopted homelands.

How did British control of India spread Sikhism?
_____
_____
_____
_____
_____

CHALLENGE ACTIVITY

Critical Thinking: Analyze Analyze Sikhism's belief that all people are equal before God. How do Sikhs demonstrate this belief, and yet also observe the caste system? Write a short paragraph explaining your answer.

raised large stone pillars carved with Buddhist **edicts,** or laws. When Asoka died, however, his sons struggled for power and foreign invaders threatened the country. The Mauryan Empire fell in 184 BC. India divided into smaller states once again.

GUPTA RULERS PROMOTE HINDUISM

During the AD 300s, the Gupta dynasty united and built the prosperity of India. The Guptas were devout Hindus and encouraged the revival of Hindu traditions and writings. They also supported Jainism and Buddhism. Indian civilization reached a high point under Chandra Gupta II. He strengthened the empire's economy and borders. He also promoted the arts, literature, and religion. The Guptas believed the caste system supported stability. The role of women was very restricted. Women were expected to marry and raise children. A woman had to obey her husband and had few rights. The Gupta dynasty lasted until it was invaded by Huns from Central Asia. India broke up once again into a patchwork of small states.

> **What religions did the Gupta rulers encourage and support?**
>
> _____
>
> _____
>
> _____

THE MUGHAL EMPIRE

About 1,000 years after the end of the Gupta Empire, Turkish Muslims from Central Asia built the Mughal Empire. An emperor named Akbar instituted a tolerant religious policy. The Mughals spread Islam through the lands they conquered, but Akbar encouraged members of all religions to live and work together. Under Akbar, Muslims and Hindus in the empire lived in peace. Their cooperation created a unique Mughal culture that blended Persian, Islamic, and Hindu elements. The Mughals were known for their architecture, particularly the Taj Mahal. A later Mughal emperor reversed Akbar's

> **Underline the sentence that describes Mughal culture.**

tolerant policies, and violent revolts led to the end of the Mughal Empire.

INDIAN ACHIEVEMENTS

During the Gupta and Mauryan periods, religion influenced the arts. Many paintings and sculptures illustrated the teachings of either Hinduism or Buddhism. Beautiful Hindu and Buddhist temples were built during this time and decorated with elaborate wood and stone carvings. Great works of literature were written in Sanskrit during the Gupta dynasty. The best-known works are the *Mahabharata* and the *Ramayana*. Both of these works are still popular across the world.

> Which religions influenced the arts during the Gupta and Mauryan periods?
>
> _____
>
> _____

The ancient Indians were pioneers of **metallurgy,** the science of working with metals. Their knowledge allowed them to create high-quality tools and weapons. They also used processes for creating **alloys.** Alloys can be stronger or easier to work with than pure metals. Indian iron was very hard and pure, and Indian steel has been a valued export for centuries. In medicine, Indians developed the technique of **inoculation.** Doctors also performed some surgeries. The numbers we use today, called **Hindu-Arabic numerals,** were first developed by Indian mathematicians. They also created the concept of zero, upon which all modern math is based.

> What are two ways that early Indian mathematicians influenced modern mathematics?
>
> _____
>
> _____
>
> _____
>
> _____
>
> _____

The Indian Subcontinent

MAIN IDEAS

1. Advanced civilizations and powerful empires shaped the early history of India.
2. Powerful empires controlled India for hundreds of years.
3. Independence from Great Britain led to the division of India into several countries.
4. Indian culture is shaped by many things, including religion and a caste system.
5. Daily life in India is centered around cities, villages, and religion.
6. Today India faces many challenges, including a growing population and economic development.

Key Terms and Places

Delhi site of former Muslim kingdom in northern India

colony territory inhabited and controlled by people from a foreign land

partition division

Hinduism one of the world's oldest religions; the dominant religion of India

Buddhism religion based on the teaching of Siddhartha Gautama, the Buddha

Jainism ancient religion that teaches nonviolence as a way of life

Sikhism religion blending Hinduism and Islam and teaching equality for all

caste system divides Indian society into groups based on birth or occupation

Mumbai (Bombay) one of India's largest cities

Kolkata (Calcutta) one of India's largest cities

urbanization increase in the percentage of people who live in cities

green revolution program that encouraged farmers to adopt modern agricultural methods

Lesson Summary
EARLY CIVILIZATIONS AND EMPIRES

The Harappan civilization flourished in Pakistan's Indus River Valley between 3000 and 1700 BC. Later, an Aryan language called Sanskrit became the basis for many languages in northern India. Most of the subcontinent was conquered by the Mauryan people. After the death of Asoka, one of the greatest Mauryan

> Underline the name of one of the greatest Mauryan emperors.

rulers, the empire split up. The Gupta Empire united most of northern India. Trade and culture thrived under the Gupta rulers.

POWERFUL EMPIRES

Powerful empires controlled India for much of its history. First the Mughal Empire and then the British Empire ruled India for hundreds of years. Turkish Muslims set up a kingdom at **Delhi** in northern India and formed the Mughal Empire. Trade and culture flourished during this period, especially under Akbar, one of India's greatest rulers. As Mughal power faded, Great Britain's presence in the region increased. By the mid-1800s, India was a British **colony.**

INDEPENDENCE AND DIVISION

Under British rule, Indians were treated as second-class citizens. Mohandas Gandhi led nonviolent protests to gain Indian independence. Muslims were afraid they would have little say in a Hindu-controlled India. To avoid civil war, the British agreed to the **partition** of India. Two independent countries, India and Pakistan, were formed in 1947. Later, Sri Lanka and Maldives gained their independence from Great Britain and Bangladesh broke away from Pakistan.

> **Why was India divided into two independent countries?**
> _____
> _____
> _____
> _____
> _____

INDIAN CULTURE

India is the birthplace of several major religions. These include **Hinduism, Buddhism, Jainism,** and **Sikhism.** India's **caste system** began to develop in ancient times. The castes had rules about how their members interacted with people from other castes. Although caste discrimination is banned in India today, the Untouchables, or Dalits, still face obstacles.

> **How does the caste system impact Dalits today?**
> _____
> _____
> _____
> _____

The Indian Subcontinent

 MAIN IDEAS
1. Many different ethnic groups and religions influence the culture of India's neighbors.
2. Rapid population growth, ethnic conflicts, and environmental threats are major challenges to the region today.

Key Terms and Places

Sherpas ethnic group from the mountains of Nepal

Kashmir region which both India and Pakistan claim control over

Dhaka capital of Bangladesh and its largest city

Kathmandu capital of Nepal and its largest city

Lesson Summary
CULTURE

India's neighbors have different ways of life. Their cultures reflect the customs of many ethnic groups. For example, the **Sherpas** in Nepal often serve as guides through the Himalayas. Many of the Tamils in Sri Lanka came from India to work on plantations.

People of the region also have different religious beliefs. Like India, most of its neighbors have one major religion. For example, most people in Pakistan and Bangladesh practice Islam. Hinduism is the major religion in Nepal while Buddhism is the major religion in Sri Lanka and Bhutan.

> Circle the countries of the Indian subcontinent where most people practice Islam.

THE REGION TODAY

Since its creation in 1947, Pakistan has not had a stable government. Rebellions and assassinations have hurt the country. Pakistan also faces the challenges of overpopulation and poverty. These challenges could cause even more instability. Pakistan has also clashed with India over control of the territory of **Kashmir.** Pakistan controls

> What challenges does Pakistan face?
> _____
> _____
> _____
> _____
> _____

western Kashmir and India controls the east, but both countries claim control over the whole region.

Since 2001 Pakistan has helped the United States fight terrorism. Many people, though, think terrorists still remain in Pakistan.

Bangladesh is a small country but one of the world's most densely populated. It has about 3,279 people per square mile (1,266 per square km). More than 17 million people live in Bangladesh's capital, **Dhaka.** One of the country's main challenges is flooding from rivers and monsoons, which often causes heavy damage. For example, one flood left over 25 million people homeless.

> **Underline the sentence that tells one of Bangladesh's main challenges.**

Nepal's population is growing rapidly. Its largest city and capital, **Kathmandu,** is poor and overcrowded. Nepal also faces environmental threats. Land cleared to grow food causes deforestation. This leads to soil erosion and harms wildlife. Tourists harm its environment by leaving trash behind and using valuable resources.

> **What are two causes of damage to Nepal's environment?**
> _____
> _____
> _____

Bhutan is a small, isolated mountain kingdom between India and China. After years of isolation, Bhutan formed ties with Great Britain and India in the 1900s. Bhutan has begun to modernize, building new roads, schools, and hospitals. Most of its people are farmers, growing rice, potatoes, and corn. To protect its environment and way of life, Bhutan limits the number of tourists who may visit.

> **Underline the crops Bhutan's farmers grow.**

Sri Lanka has been greatly influenced by its close neighbor, India. Two of Sri Lanka's main ethnic groups—the Tamil and the Sinhalese—have Indian roots. The Tamil minority has fought for years to create a separate state. The fighting ended in 2009 when the government defeated the Tamils. In 2004, an Indian Ocean tsunami struck Sri Lanka, killing thousands. More than 500,000

> **Circle the two main ethnic groups in Sri Lanka.**

China's first writing system. Today's Chinese symbols are based on those of the Shang period. Shang artisans made bronze containers and ornaments, knives, and axes from jade.

ZHOU AND QIN DYNASTIES

The Zhou (JOH) dynasty replaced the Shang in the 1100s BC. It became the longest-lasting dynasty in Chinese history. The Zhou believed in the **mandate of heaven**, the idea that heaven chose China's rulers. They also established a new political order. The emperor was at the top of society. He gave land to lords who were loyal or who served in the military. Peasants who farmed the land were below lords.

Important thinkers developed new beliefs. Laozi founded Daoism (DOW-ih-zum). Daoism taught that people should live in harmony with nature and with each other. Another great teacher was Confucius. He taught the importance of moral values such as respect and loyalty. He believed that people should know their proper roles in society and that rulers should be examples of good behavior. Many people adopted the ideas of these teachers.

In 771 BC the emperor was overthrown and China entered a time called the Warring States period. In 221 BC a king from the state called Qin defeated all others and unified China. He gave himself the title Shi Huangdi (SHEE hwahng-dee), which means "first emperor." Shi Huangdi took land away from the lords and forced noble families to move to his capital, now called **Xi'an** (SHEE-AHN). He set up a new system of laws and made China's money and writing the same everywhere. The Qin built a network of roads and canals. They also built the **Great Wall** to protect China from northern invaders. China began to break apart after Shi Huangdi's death.

> Who was at the top of the Zhou political system? Who was at the bottom?
>
> _____
>
> _____

THE HAN DYNASTY

After years of fighting, Liu Bang (lee-OO bang) established the Han dynasty. He lowered taxes for farmers and reduced punishments. He also depended on educated officials to help him rule. Later, the emperor Wudi (WOO-dee) made Confucianism the official government philosophy of China. To get a government job, a person had to pass a test based on Confucian teachings. However, wealthy and influential families still controlled the government.

The Han organized society into classes based on the Confucian system. The emperor, his court, and scholars made up the upper class. The peasants were the second class, followed by artisans. Merchants were the lowest class because they did not actually produce anything. Wealthy people lived on large estates and peasants worked their land. Peasants were the largest class but most were poor. Confucian ideas about the family were promoted. Children were taught to respect their elders. The father was the head of the family.

> Underline the phrase that explains how a person got a government job during the Han dynasty.

HAN ACHIEVEMENTS AND TRADE

The Chinese produced much art and literature during the Han dynasty. Inventors developed many useful devices. They invented paper, the **sundial**, and the **seismograph**. They also developed the medical practice of **acupuncture**. These and other Han inventions and advances are still used today.

Another achievement was the development of trade. Countries to the west wanted Chinese silk. Traders used overland routes such as the **Silk Road** to take Chinese goods to Central Asia. Traders there continued on the route as far as the Mediterranean Sea. Ideas such as papermaking techniques and religions were also exchanged. Bandits, blizzards, and sandstorms

> Circle three things that were exchanged along the Silk Road.

Lesson 2, *continued*

Wu was the only woman to rule China. After the fall of the Tang dynasty, separate kingdoms competed for power. This period, called the Five Dynasties and Ten Kingdoms, was ended by the Song dynasty. The Song ruled for about 300 years. This was a time of great economic and cultural achievements.

CITIES AND TRADE

China's growing cities were crowded with people, shops, artisans, and government officials. The largest city of the Tang dynasty, Chang'an (now called Xi'an), was a major trade center. Growth continued during the Song dynasty. **Kaifeng** (KY-fuhng), the Song capital, had about a million people. Traders used the Grand Canal to ship goods and agricultural products throughout China. Foreign trade traveled over both land routes and sea routes.

Chinese exports included tea, rice, spices, and jade. Silk and **porcelain** were especially popular in other countries. The Chinese kept the method of making silk a secret for centuries.

> **Why do you think the Chinese kept the method for making silk a secret?**
> _____
> _____
> _____

ARTS AND INVENTIONS

The Tang and Song dynasties produced great artists and writers. In addition, some of the most important inventions in human history were created. A Tang invention called **woodblock printing** produced the world's first known printed book. Later, during the Song dynasty, the Chinese invented movable type for printing. Movable type can be rearranged and reused to create new lines of text and different pages. The Song dynasty also introduced the world's first paper money. Two other Tang dynasty inventions include **gunpowder** and the **compass**. The compass revolutionized travel, and gunpowder dramatically changed how wars were fought.

> **Circle the invention that replaced woodblock printing.**

CONFUCIANISM

Confucius's teachings focused on ethics, or proper behavior, of individuals and governments. During the Period of Disunion, Buddhism overshadowed Confucianism. However, late in the Tang dynasty, scholars again turned to Confucianism. They wanted to improve Chinese government and society. During and after the Song dynasty, a new version of Confucianism developed, known as Neo-Confucianism. In addition to teaching proper behavior, Neo-Confucianism emphasized spiritual matters. These ideas became official government teachings after the Song dynasty.

> **Underline the sentence that explains what Neo-Confucianism emphasized.**

SCHOLAR-OFFICIALS

The Song dynasty improved the government workforce. Workers had to pass a series of written **civil service** examinations to work for the government **bureaucracy**. The tests covered both the teachings of Confucius and related ideas. In this way, government officials were chosen by ability instead of wealth or influence. The tests were very difficult, and students spent years preparing for them. Passing the tests meant life as a **scholar-official**. Benefits included people's respect and reduced penalties for breaking the law. The civil service examination system helped ensure that talented, intelligent people became scholar-officials. This system was a major factor in the stability of the Song government.

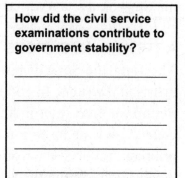

> **How did the civil service examinations contribute to government stability?**
>
> _____
> _____
> _____
> _____
> _____

CHALLENGE ACTIVITY

Critical Thinking: Make Judgments Which do you think is better: a government that gives people jobs based on test scores or one that gives people jobs based on their family connections? Explain your answer.

China, Mongolia, and Taiwan

MAIN IDEAS

1. Physical features of China, Mongolia, and Taiwan include mountains, plateaus and basins, plains, and rivers.
2. China, Mongolia, and Taiwan have a range of climates and natural resources.

Key Terms and Places

Himalayas world's tallest mountain range

Plateau of Tibet world's highest plateau, located in southwest China

Gobi world's coldest desert, located in Mongolia

North China Plain fertile plain in east China

Huang He Yellow River, a river in northern China that often floods

loess fertile, yellowish soil

Chang Jiang Yangzi River, Asia's longest river, flows across central China

Lesson Summary
PHYSICAL FEATURES

China has a range of physical features. These include the world's tallest mountains, as well as some of the world's driest deserts and longest rivers. Mongolia and Taiwan are two of China's neighbors. Mongolia is north of China. It is a dry, landlocked country with vast grasslands and desert. Taiwan is a green tropical island.

There are mountains in much of the region. The **Himalayas** run along the border of southwest China. They are the tallest mountains in the world. Mount Everest is located in this mountain range. Many of the mountain ranges are separated by plateaus, basins, and deserts. North of the Himalayas is the **Plateau of Tibet**. It is the highest plateau on Earth and is called the Roof of the World.

North of this area is the Taklimakan Desert. It is a barren land with sand dunes and sandstorms.

> **How are Mongolia and Taiwan different?**
> _____
> _____
> _____

> **Where in China are the Himalayas located?**
> _____
> _____

Another desert, the **Gobi**, is located in Mongolia. It is the world's coldest desert.

Most Chinese live in east China, where there are low plains and river valleys, such as the **North China Plain**. This fertile area has farmlands and population centers. In Taiwan, most people live on a plain on the west coast.

| Underline the region where most Chinese live. |

Two long rivers run west to east across China. The **Huang He**, or the Yellow River, picks up a fertile, yellowish soil called **loess**. The river often floods in summer and deposits the loess, enriching farmland along the banks. Many people are killed by these floods. Another river, the **Chang Jiang**, or the Yangzi River, flows across central China. It is Asia's longest river and a major transportation route.

| Why is the Chang Jiang a major transportation route? |
| _____ |
| _____ |
| _____ |

CLIMATE AND RESOURCES

Climate varies widely across the region. The tropical southeast is warm to hot. There, monsoons bring heavy rains in the summer. Violent storms called typhoons bring high winds and rain in the summer and fall. The climate in the north and west is mainly dry. Temperatures across this area vary. The climate in the northeast is quite different. It is drier and colder. In the winter, temperatures can drop below 0°F (–18°C).

| What is a typhoon? |
| _____ |
| _____ |
| _____ |

The region has a variety of natural resources. China has many resources, including minerals and metals. It is a leading producer of coal. Farmland and forestland are also important. Mongolia's natural resources include minerals and livestock. Taiwan's main resource is farmland. It grows crops such as sugarcane, tea, and bananas.

| Circle an important resource in both China and Taiwan. |

The Nationalists fled to Taiwan, where they founded the Republic of China.

Mao Zedong led the new Communist government. In a Communist system, the government owns most businesses and land and controls all areas of life. Some people's lives improved, but freedoms were limited. Many economic programs failed.

Mao died in 1976. China's next leader was Deng Xiaoping. Deng worked to modernize and improve the economy. He allowed some private businesses and let other countries invest in China. The economy began growing rapidly. Leaders after Deng continued economic reforms, but economic freedom did not lead to political freedom.

China punishes people who disagree with the government. In 1989 a huge protest took place in China's capital, **Beijing**. About 100,000 people gathered in Tiananmen Square to demand more political rights and freedoms. The government used force to make people leave the square. Many protesters were killed or imprisoned.

China has also put down ethnic rebellions. Since 1950 China has controlled **Tibet**, a Buddhist region. When Tibetans rebelled, China crushed the revolt. Tibet's Buddhist leader, the Dalai Lama, fled to India.

ECONOMY

Until the 1980s China's Communist government had a **command economy**, in which the government owns all the businesses and makes all decisions. In the 1970s China began allowing a limited market economy. In a market economy, people can decide what to make or sell and keep the profits they earn. This mixed economic approach helped China become the world's second-largest economy.

How did Deng Xiaoping change China's economy?
_____
_____
_____
_____
_____

What is China's capital city?
_____
_____

What is the government's role in a command economy?
_____
_____
_____

Only about 11 percent of China's land is good for farming. However, more than a third of workers are farmers. China is a leading producer of food crops.

China is also the largest manufacturing economy in the world. Economic growth has improved wages and living standards. More Chinese can now afford TVs, computers, and cars. Still, many rural Chinese remain poor and many cannot find work.

> **What are the two most important parts of China's economy?**
>
> _____
>
> _____

POPULATION

China has the world's largest population, with more than 1.3 billion people. Most people live in eastern China. The population grows by about 6 million people each year. The Chinese government has worked to slow this growth by urging people to delay having children and to have only one child.

Most Chinese live in small, rural villages, where farmers work the fields. Villages have small shops or people selling food and goods along the streets. Many people are moving to cities, which are growing rapidly. Most large cities are on the coast or along major rivers. Industry and trade contribute to their growth.

China's largest city is **Shanghai**, located where the Chang Jiang meets the East China Sea. Shanghai is China's leading seaport and an industrial and commercial center. Beijing is the second-largest city. It is China's political and cultural center. **Hong Kong** and Macao (muh-KOW) are important port cities in southern China. They are modern centers of trade and tourism.

> **Why is Shanghai a leading seaport?**
>
> _____
>
> _____
>
> _____

ENVIRONMENT

China's growth has created serious environmental problems. The country's growing number of cars and factories pollute the air and water. Burning

China, Mongolia, and Taiwan

MAIN IDEAS
1. Mongolia is a sparsely populated country where many people live as nomads.
2. Taiwan is a small island with a dense population and a highly industrialized economy.

Key Terms and Places

gers large, circular, felt tents that are easy to put up, take down, and move

Ulaanbaatar Mongolia's capital and only large city

Taipei Taiwan's capital and main financial center

Kao-hsiung Taiwan's main seaport and a center of heavy industry

Lesson Summary
MONGOLIA

The people of Mongolia have a proud and fascinating history. About 700 years ago, Mongolia was perhaps the greatest power in the world. Under the ruler Genghis Khan, Mongols conquered much of Asia, including China. Eventually, their empire stretched from Europe eastward to the Pacific Ocean. Over time, the empire declined. China conquered Mongolia in the late 1600s.

Mongolia declared independence from China in 1911. The Communists gained control in 1924. The Soviet Union helped Mongolia economically and was a strong influence. This help ended after the Soviet Union collapsed in 1991. Since then, Mongolians have tried to build a democratic government and a free-market economy.

Many Mongolians follow a traditional way of life. Nearly half live as nomads, herding livestock. Many live in **gers**. These large, circular, felt tents are easy to put up, take down, and move. Horses play a major role in nomadic life.

Mongolia is large but has a small population of only about 3 million people. More than a

> Who was the leader who built Mongolia's empire?
>
> _____

> Circle the name of the country that strongly influenced Mongolia.

> How do about half of Mongolians live?
>
> _____
>
> _____

quarter of them live in **Ulaanbaatar**, Mongolia's capital and only large city. It is the main industrial and commercial center.

What is Mongolia's capital city?

The country's main industries include textiles, carpets, coal, copper, and oil. Mongolia produces livestock but very little other food.

TAIWAN

Both China and Japan controlled Taiwan at different times. In 1949 the Chinese Nationalists took over the island. Led by Chang Kai-shek, they fled the Chinese mainland when the Communists took control. The Nationalists ruled Taiwan under martial law, or military rule, for 38 years. Today, Taiwan's government is a multiparty democracy.

What group came to Taiwan after the Communists took over mainland China?

Taiwan functions as an independent country, but there is still tension between China and Taiwan. China claims Taiwan is a rebel part of China. Taiwan claims to be China's true government.

Taiwan's population is about 85 percent native Taiwanese. They are descended from Chinese people who came to Taiwan in the 1700s and 1800s. As a result, Chinese ways are an important part of Taiwan's culture. In larger cities, some people follow European and American customs.

What is the major cultural influence in Taiwan?

Taiwan is a modern country with about 23 million people. Most Taiwanese live in cities on the island's western coastal plain. The rest of the country is mountainous. The two largest cities are **Taipei** and **Kao-hsiung**. Taipei is Taiwan's capital and main financial center. Kao-hsiung is a center of heavy industry and Taiwan's main seaport.

Underline the place where most Taiwanese live.

Taiwan is one of Asia's richest countries. It has a lot of industries, including making computers and sports equipment. Farmers grow many crops, including sugarcane.

> **MAIN IDEAS**
> 1. Japan's early government was ruled by emperors and shoguns.
> 2. Japanese culture blends traditional customs with modern innovations.
> 3. Since World War II, Japan has developed a democratic government.
> 4. Japan has become one of the world's strongest economies.
> 5. A shortage of open space shapes daily life in Japan.
> 6. Crowding, competition, and pollution are among Japan's main issues and challenges.

Key Terms and Places

Kyoto Japan's imperial capital, known before as Heian

shoguns powerful military leaders of imperial Japan

samurai highly trained warriors

kimonos traditional Japanese robes

Diet Japan's elected legislature

Tokyo capital of Japan

work ethic belief that work in itself is worthwhile

trade surplus exists when a country exports more goods than it imports

tariff fee a country charges for exports or imports

Osaka Japan's second-largest city

Lesson Summary
HISTORY

Japan lies across the sea from China, so Chinese culture has been an important influence. One example is Buddhism, which became Japan's main religion. Japan's first government was modeled after China's. Both countries were ruled by emperors. Japan's emperors made their capital in Heian (now called **Kyoto**), a center for the arts.

Eventually, the emperors' power slipped away. Japan fell under the control of powerful generals called **shoguns**. One shogun would rule in the emperor's name. Shoguns had armies of fierce warriors called **samurai**. The shoguns ruled Japan

> Who took government power away from the emperors of Japan?
>
> _____

until 1868, when a group of samurai gave power back to the emperor.

During World War II, Japan sided with Germany and Italy. It wanted to build an empire in Southeast Asia and the Pacific. Japan brought the United States into the war in 1941, when it bombed the naval base at Pearl Harbor. To end the war, the Americans dropped atomic bombs on the Japanese cities of Hiroshima and Nagasaki. These powerful weapons caused Japan to surrender.

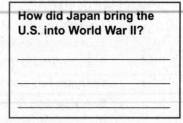

How did Japan bring the U.S. into World War II?

JAPANESE CULTURE

Some Japanese culture is influenced by China, but many elements are native to Japan. Western culture is also an important influence.

Nearly everyone in Japan speaks Japanese, a difficult language to learn. The Japanese writing system uses two types of characters. Some characters, called kanji, represent a single word. About 2,000 kanji characters are commonly used. Other characters, called kana, stand for a part of a word.

Circle the names of the kinds of characters used to write Japanese.

Most Japanese people combine elements of Shinto and Buddhism in their religious practices. Shinto is native to Japan. In the Shinto religion, everything in nature is believed to have a spirit, or *kami*. Buddhism encourages people to seek enlightenment and peace. There are many Shinto and Buddhist shrines and temples in Japan.

Most people in Japan wear Western-style clothing, but many also wear traditional **kimonos** on special occasions. Traditional forms of art include Noh and Kabuki plays.

What do Japanese people wear most of the time?

GOVERNMENT

Japan's government has changed since World War II, and it is now a democracy. Although Japan's emperor is the country's official leader, he has little power. His main role is to act as a symbol of Japan. In Japan today, power rests with an elected legislature called the **Diet**. The Diet chooses a prime minister. The seat of government and capital of Japan is **Tokyo**.

Circle the words that explain who has power in Japan.

ECONOMY

Until the 1950s the Japanese economy was not strong. But within a few decades, Japan became an economic powerhouse. It is the home of successful companies like Honda, Toyota, and Sony. Japanese companies are known for manufacturing high-quality products, and they are leaders in creating new technology.

The government has helped Japanese companies succeed by controlling production and planning for the future. Workers are highly trained and have a strong **work ethic**, which also helps.

Japan's economy depends on trade. Many goods made in Japan are intended for export to other countries. The United States is Japan's main trading partner. Japan exports much more than it imports, causing a huge **trade surplus**. This has added to Japan's wealth. Japanese people do not buy many imported goods because a high **tariff**, or fee, makes them expensive.

What happens to many of the goods manufactured in Japan?
_____
_____

Japan's economic success is due to its manufacturing, not natural resources. Japan must import most of the raw materials it uses to make goods. Since there is little farmland, Japan must also import much of its food from countries like China and the United States.

DAILY LIFE

Tokyo is the center of Japan's banking and communication industries. Like most Japanese cities, it is densely populated and very crowded. Almost 36 million people live in the Tokyo area, making land scarce and expensive.

About how many people live in the Tokyo area?
_____

Tokyo has tall, narrow buildings that use less land area. There are shops and restaurants in subway stations underground. Some hotels save space by housing guests in tiny sleeping chambers rather than rooms. Many people commute to Tokyo from outside the city. Trains are often jammed with commuters.

Other cities include **Osaka**, Japan's second-largest city located in western Honshu, and Kyoto, the former capital. Kyoto is full of historic buildings. Japan's major cities are linked by efficient, high-speed trains called bullet trains, which can reach more than 160 miles per hour (260 kph). Most people live in cities, but some live in villages or on farms. Many farmers have left rural areas to find jobs in cities.

ISSUES AND CHALLENGES

Japan's lack of space is a growing problem. Housing is crowded, commutes are long, and new tall buildings must withstand earthquakes.

> Underline three reasons lack of space is a challenge.

Japan also faces economic competition from countries such as China and South Korea, whose companies have taken away Japanese business. Many Japanese companies are decades old. To compete, the country must create new businesses.

There are also environmental concerns. Pollution is a problem. In 1997 the Kyoto Protocol agreement was signed by 150 countries to help cut pollution and improve air quality. And in 2011 a massive earthquake struck Japan, causing a tsunami that killed more than 18,000 people. It created a dangerous meltdown in a nuclear power plant. Today, the Japanese continue to rebuild their nation.

> What is the Kyoto Protocol?
>
> _____
> _____
> _____
> _____

Lesson 3, *continued*

The Soviet Union helped Communists take control in North Korea, while the United States helped to form a democratic government in South Korea. In 1950 North Korea invaded the south, starting the Korean War. North Korea wanted to unite Korea under a Communist government. The United States helped South Korea remain separate.

> **What action started the Korean War?**
> _____
> _____

KOREAN CULTURE

People in both North and South Korea speak Korean. Unlike Japanese, written Korean uses an alphabet. Korea's traditional religion is shamanism. However, today, Christianity is the most widely practiced religion in South Korea. Buddhism is second. Communist North Korea discourages people from practicing any religion.

The people of Korea have kept many old customs. **Kimchi**, a spicy dish made from pickled cabbage, has been eaten for centuries. Traditions are especially important in North Korea, where the Communists want to preserve the country's customs and culture. In South Korea, people in rural areas keep their traditional ways. However, people in cities have adopted modern ways of life.

> **What parts of North and South Korea are more likely to keep traditions?**
> _____
> _____
> _____

SOUTH KOREA TODAY

The official name of South Korea is the Republic of Korea. It is a democracy, headed by a president and an assembly. Both are elected by the people. After World War II, the United States helped create South Korea's government and gave it economic support. In the first half of the 20th century, South Korea was poor. Today, it has one of the strongest economies in East Asia. It is a major manufacturing country that exports goods around the world.

Like Japan, South Korea is densely populated. Its capital, **Seoul**, is one of the most densely populated cities in the world. It has more than

> **Underline the official name of South Korea.**

44,000 people per square mile. The most crowded part of the country is on the western coast.

In the cities, people live in small apartments. Housing is expensive, and there is pollution. In the country, many South Koreans live on small farms, grow rice, beans, and cabbage, and are more traditional.

Although South Korea has a strong economy, many people feel that its government is corrupt. For many years, four families controlled much of the country's industry, which gave them wealth and power. In 2016 the president was impeached due to a scandal related to these businesses.

A big challenge for South Korea is its relationship with North Korea. Since the end of the Korean War in the 1950s, the countries have been separated by a **demilitarized zone**. This empty area has no soldiers but is patrolled by guards on both sides to keep the countries from fighting.

> **Why is there a demilitarized zone between North and South Korea?**
>
> _____
> _____
> _____

NORTH KOREA TODAY

North Korea's official name, the Democratic People's Republic of Korea, is misleading. The country is not democratic. It is a totalitarian, Communist state.

From 1948 until 1994, it was led by the dictator Kim Il Sung. At Kim's death, his son, Kim Jong Il, became ruler. He was called "Dear Leader" by North Koreans, but he was a brutal dictator. Under his rule, North Koreans suffered human rights abuses, poverty, and widespread hunger. He developed weapons to threaten neighboring countries. After Kim Jong Il's death in 2011, his son Kim Jong Un took over. There was hope he would improve life for North Koreans. However, he followed his father's policies.

> **When did Kim Il Sung rule North Korea?**
>
> _____

North Korea has a command economy. In this economy, the government makes all economic decisions. It also owns all land and controls all

Southeast Asia

MAIN IDEAS
1. Southeast Asia's physical features include peninsulas, islands, rivers, and many seas, straits, and gulfs.
2. The tropical climate of Southeast Asia supports a wide range of plants and animals.
3. Southeast Asia is rich in natural resources such as wood, rubber, and fossil fuels.

Key Terms and Places

Indochina Peninsula peninsula that makes up part of Mainland Southeast Asia

Malay Peninsula peninsula that makes up part of Mainland Southeast Asia

Malay Archipelago island group that makes up part of Island Southeast Asia

archipelago large group of islands

New Guinea Earth's second-largest island

Borneo Earth's third-largest island

Mekong River most important river in Southeast Asia

Lesson Summary
PHYSICAL FEATURES

Two peninsulas and two large island groups make up the Southeast Asia region. Mainland Southeast Asia is made up of the **Indochina Peninsula** and the **Malay Peninsula**. Island Southeast Asia is made up of the many islands of the Philippines and the **Malay Archipelago**. An **archipelago** is a large group of islands.

Mainland Southeast Asia includes the countries of Myanmar, Thailand, Laos, and Vietnam. This region has rugged mountains, low plateaus, and river floodplains. Island Southeast Asia has more than 20,000 islands. These include **New Guinea**, the world's second-largest island, and **Borneo**, the world's third-largest island. Some of the larger islands have high mountains with snow and glaciers.

> Underline the two peninsulas that make up Mainland Southeast Asia.

Lesson 1, *continued*

Island Southeast Asia is part of the Ring of Fire, where earthquakes and volcanoes often occur. Underwater earthquakes can cause giant waves called tsunamis. In 2004 a tsunami in the Indian Ocean killed hundreds of thousands of people, many in Southeast Asia.

What is the Ring of Fire?
_____
_____

Southeast Asia has many water bodies, such as seas, straits, and gulfs. Several major rivers drain the mainland's peninsulas. The **Mekong River** is the most important river. The region's fertile river valleys and deltas support farming and are home to many people.

CLIMATE, PLANTS, AND ANIMALS

Southeast Asia is in the tropics, the area on and around the equator. This region is generally warm to hot all year round. It is cooler in the north and in the mountains.

Much of the mainland has a tropical savanna climate. Savannas—areas of tall grasses and some trees and shrubs—grow here. Monsoon winds from the ocean bring heavy rain in summer and drier weather in winter. Wet seasons often have severe flooding.

Where do monsoon winds come from?
_____

The islands and the Malay Peninsula have a mostly humid tropical climate. It is hot, muggy, and rainy all year, with daily storms. Huge storms, called typhoons, can bring heavy rain and powerful winds.

This humid climate supports tropical rain forests. These forests are home to many different plants and animals. Indonesia alone has about 40,000 kinds of flowering plants. There are also many animals, including elephants, monkeys, tigers, and birds. Animals such as orangutans and Komodo dragons are found only in this region. Many of these plants and animals are endangered. Their habitat, the rain forest, is being cut down for timber, farming, and mining.

Why are the plants and animals of the rain forest endangered?
_____
_____
_____

MAIN IDEAS
1. Southeast Asia's early history includes empires, colonial rule, and independence.
2. The modern history of Southeast Asia involves struggles with war and communism.
3. Southeast Asia's culture reflects its Chinese, Indian, and European heritage.
4. The area today is largely rural and agricultural, but cities are growing rapidly.
5. Myanmar is poor with a harsh military government, while Thailand is a democracy with a strong economy.
6. The countries of Indochina are poor and struggling to rebuild after years of war.

Key Terms and Places

Timor small island that stayed under Portugal's control after the Dutch took over the region

domino theory idea that if one country fell to communism, other countries nearby would follow like falling dominoes

wats Buddhist temples that also serve as monasteries

Yangon Myanmar's capital and major seaport

human rights rights that all people deserve, such as rights to equality and justice

Bangkok capital and largest city of Thailand

klongs canals

Phnom Penh Cambodia's capital and chief city

Hanoi capital of Vietnam, located in the north

Lesson Summary
EARLY HISTORY

China and India lie close to Southeast Asia and have had a strong role in its history. Many people from China and India settled in Southeast Asia, creating trade between the countries.

According to recent research, humans lived in Southeast Asia's rain forests as long as 11,000 years ago. The most advanced early civilization was the Khmer. Their empire lasted from the AD 800s to the mid-1200s in what is now Cambodia. The Khmer built a huge temple, Angkor Wat. This temple is an example of their advanced civilization and Hindu religion. In the 1200s the Thai came from southern China and settled in the Khmer area. Buddhism began to replace Hinduism in the region.

Starting in the 1500s, European countries came to the area to colonize, trade, and spread their religion. Portugal led the way. Spain claimed the Philippines and spread Roman Catholicism there. Later, the Dutch drove Portugal out of much of the region. Portugal kept **Timor**, a small island, but the Dutch controlled the tea and spice trade in what is now Indonesia.

> **Why did European countries come to this region?**
> _____
> _____
> _____

In the 1800s the British and French set up colonies with plantations, railroads, and mines. People from China and India worked in the colonies. The British and French also spread Christianity. In 1898 the United States came into the region when it won the Philippines from Spain in the Spanish-American War. Colonial powers ruled all of the area except for Siam (now Thailand) by the early 1900s.

> **Circle the year the United States entered the region.**

During World War II, Japan invaded and occupied most of Southeast Asia. When the war ended, the United States granted the Philippines independence. Other countries in the region started to fight for independence, too. The French left Indochina in 1954 after a bloody war. The independent countries of Cambodia, Laos, and Vietnam were formed from this area. By 1970 most of Southeast Asia was free from colonial rule.

> **What three countries were formed from Indochina?**
> _____
> _____
> _____

MODERN HISTORY

In Vietnam, feelings of nationalism, or loyalty to the country, led to the fight against French colonialism. The Vietnamese were led by

Ho Chi Minh, a Communist. The fighting divided the country into North and South Vietnam. In South Vietnam, a civil war started.

In the 1960s the United States decided to send troops to South Vietnam to fight Communist forces. This decision was based on the **domino theory**—the idea that if one country fell to communism, other nearby countries would fall, too. Years of war led to millions of deaths and terrible destruction. Eventually, North and South Vietnam became one Communist country. About a million refugees fled. Many went to the United States.

Civil wars also broke out in Cambodia and Laos. In 1975 Communists took over both countries. Cambodia's government was brutal. Vietnam helped overthrow Cambodia's government in 1978. Fighting lasted until the mid-1990s.

Restate the domino theory in your own words.
_____
_____
_____
_____
_____
_____

CULTURE

Southeast Asia blends native, Chinese, Indian, and European cultures. There are hundreds of ethnic groups in the region. There are also many languages and religions. Buddhism is the most popular religion on the mainland. The area is home to many beautiful Buddhist temples, or **wats**, which also serve as monasteries. Islam is the main religion in Malaysia, Brunei, and Indonesia. Indonesia has more Muslims than any other country. In the Philippines, most people are Roman Catholic. The island of Bali and Indian communities practice Hinduism.

Circle the four main religions practiced in Southeast Asia.

Customs vary widely, yet there are some similarities. Religion and religious festivals are important parts of daily life. Traditional dances and music are still popular, especially in rural areas. Also, many people still wear traditional clothing such as sarongs, strips of cloth worn wrapped around the body.

MAINLAND SOUTHEAST ASIA TODAY

Mainland Southeast Asia includes the countries
of Myanmar, Thailand, Cambodia, Laos, and
Vietnam. Because of war, harsh governments,
and other problems, progress has slowed in much
of this area. However, the area's rich resources
make the future promising. In 2010 most of the
countries of Southeast Asia joined the
Association of Southeast Asian Nations
(ASEAN). It promotes political, economic, and
social cooperation in the region.

Most of Mainland Southeast Asia is rural and
most people are farmers. They live in small
villages and grow rice. Most farm work is done
using traditional methods.

Mainland Southeast Asia has several big cities.
They are growing rapidly as people move to them
in search of work.

MYANMAR AND THAILAND

Myanmar, also called Burma, is a poor country.
It gained independence from Great Britain in
1948. **Yangon**, or Rangoon, is its capital, though
the administrative capital is Naypyidaw. Most
people in Myanmar are Burmese. Many live in
small farming villages, with houses built on stilts.
The main religion is Buddhism.

For about half a century, a harsh military
government has ruled Myanmar. This
government abuses **human rights**—rights that all
people deserve. One woman, Aung San Suu Kyi,
has led a movement for more democracy and
rights. She and others have been repeatedly
arrested. Her fight for reform resulted in the
country's first free elections in 2016.

Thailand, once called Siam, has the area's
strongest economy. Its capital and largest city is
Bangkok. It is a modern, crowded city, which lies
near the mouth of the Chao Phraya River.
Bangkok is known for its palaces and Buddhist

Who is Aung San Suu Kyi?
_____
_____
_____
_____

Southeast Asia

MAIN IDEAS
1. The area today has rich resources and growing cities but faces challenges.
2. Malaysia and its neighbors have strong economies but differ in many ways.
3. Indonesia and the Philippines are diverse with growing economies, and East Timor is small and poor.

Key Terms and Places

Timor-Leste small island of Timor that declared independence from Indonesia in 1999

kampongs villages or city districts with traditional houses built on stilts; slums around cities

Jakarta capital of Indonesia

Kuala Lumpur Malaysia's capital and a cultural and economic center

free ports ports that place few, if any, taxes on goods

sultan supreme ruler of a Muslim country

Java Indonesia's main island

Manila capital of the Philippines

Lesson Summary
THE AREA TODAY

The six countries of Island Southeast Asia are Malaysia, Singapore, Brunei, Indonesia, **Timor-Leste**, and the Philippines. These countries could have bright futures. They have rich resources and skilled labor forces. Their economies are growing. All but Timor-Leste belong to ASEAN, which promotes cooperation in Southeast Asia.

However, these island countries still face challenges. Ethnic conflicts have hurt progress. Many people live in poverty, while much of the money is controlled by only a few leaders and businesspeople. There are many environmental problems, such as pollution.

> Underline three challenges facing Island Southeast Asia.

Many people in Island Southeast Asia live in rural areas. They fish or farm. Seafood is the main source of protein. Rice is the main crop, though they also grow coffee, spices, sugarcane, tea, and tropical fruit. Indonesia and Malaysia are the world's biggest producers of rubber.

As on the mainland, many people here are moving to cities for work. The capitals are the largest cities. They are modern and crowded. Common problems include smog, heavy traffic, and large slums. In some areas, people live in **kampongs**, places with traditional houses on stilts. The stilts protect houses from flooding. The term *kampong* also refers to slums in cities such as **Jakarta**, Indonesia's capital.

Why might people want to live in a house on stilts?
_____
_____

MALAYSIA AND ITS NEIGHBORS

Malaysia has two parts. One part is on the island of Borneo. The other is on the southern part of the Malay Peninsula. This is where most Malaysians live. Malaysia's capital, **Kuala Lumpur**, is also located there. Kuala Lumpur is the country's cultural and economic center.

Circle the two areas that make up Malaysia.

Malaysia is ethnically diverse. Malays are the main ethnic group, but many Chinese and other groups live there, too. This is why the country has many languages and religions. Bahasa Malay is the main language. Islam and Buddhism are the main religions.

Malaysia is a constitutional monarchy. Local rulers take turns being king, which is mostly a ceremonial position. A prime minister and elected legislature hold the real power. The country has one of the strongest economies in the region. It has well-educated workers and rich resources. It produces and exports natural rubber, palm oil, electronics, oil, and timber.

Singapore is on a tiny island at the tip of the Malay Peninsula. This location is on a major shipping route, which has made Singapore rich.

How does Singapore's location help its economy?
_____
_____

It is one of the world's busiest **free ports**—ports with few or no taxes on goods. Singapore is also an industrial center with many offices of foreign banks and high-tech firms. The city is modern, wealthy, orderly, and clean.

Singapore has a low crime rate, but that is because of strict laws. The government has cleaned up slums and improved housing. But it also gives fines for littering. People caught with illegal drugs can be executed. Politics and media are also controlled by the government.

Brunei is a tiny country on Borneo. It is ruled by a **sultan**, the supreme ruler of a Muslim country. Large oil and gas deposits have made Brunei wealthy. This wealth allows citizens to receive free health care and other benefits. They do not pay taxes. However, the oil is expected to run out around 2020, so the government is trying to find other ways to develop the economy.

Why does Singapore have a low crime rate?
_____
_____

Underline the text that explains the economic problem soon facing Brunei.

INDONESIA, TIMOR-LESTE, AND THE PHILIPPINES

Indonesia is the world's largest archipelago, with over 13,500 islands. It has the fourth-largest population of any country and the world's largest Muslim population. The country has more than 300 ethnic groups that speak over 250 languages.

Java is Indonesia's main island. The capital, Jakarta, is there. More than half the population live in Java, making it extremely crowded. To reduce the crowding, the government is moving people to less-populated islands. This is an unpopular policy.

Indonesia has rich resources, such as rubber, oil, gas, and timber. There is good farmland for rice and other crops. Factories and tourism also help the economy. But there are also problems. People are poor and unemployment is high. In some areas, religious and ethnic conflicts have led to violence.

Timor-Leste is on the small island of Timor. In 1999 Timor-Leste declared independence from Indonesia, leading to years of violence. The United Nations sent in troops to end the war. The fighting left Timor-Leste poor. Most people farm, and coffee is the main export.

What led to the war in Timor-Leste?
_____
_____

The Philippines has more than 7,000 islands. The largest is Luzon. It is the most populated island, and the capital, **Manila**, is there. The Philippines is one of the most diverse countries in the region. It is home to ten ethnic groups and many foreigners.

The country's many natural resources include metals, oil, and woods. Farming and manufacturing are also important for the economy. However, even though the economy has improved, there is a big gap between the rich and poor. Few Filipinos are wealthy. Most are poor farmers who do not own any land.

What is one of the main economic problems in the Philippines?
_____
_____
_____

The country is mainly Roman Catholic, but some areas are mostly Muslim. These areas want independence. This has led to violent conflicts.

CHALLENGE ACTIVITY

Critical Thinking: Draw Inferences Choose two island countries of Southeast Asia and write a paragraph that compares two of the following categories: geography, people, government, economy.

MAIN IDEAS

1. Unique physical features, tropical climates, and limited resources shape the physical geography of the Pacific Islands.
2. Native customs and contact with the Western world have influenced the history and culture of the Pacific Islands.
3. Pacific Islanders today are working to improve their economies and protect the environment.

Key Terms and Places

Micronesia region of Pacific Islands located east of the Philippines

Melanesia region of Pacific Islands stretching from New Guinea to Fiji

Polynesia largest region of Pacific Islands, east of Melanesia

atolls small, ring-shaped coral islands surrounding lagoons

territory area that is under the control of another government

Lesson Summary
PHYSICAL GEOGRAPHY

There are three regions of islands in the Pacific. **Micronesia**, consisting of about 2,000 small islands, is east of the Philippines. **Melanesia**, the most heavily populated region, stretches from New Guinea to Fiji. **Polynesia**, the largest region, is located east of Melanesia and includes Tonga, Samoa, and the Hawaiian Islands.

There are two kinds of islands in the Pacific: high islands and low islands. High islands are formed from volcanoes or continental rock. They tend to be mountainous and rocky. They have dense forests, rich soil, and many mineral resources. Low islands are much smaller; they have thin soil, little vegetation, few resources, and low elevations. Many low islands are **atolls**, small, ring-shaped coral islands surrounding lagoons.

Most high and low islands have a humid tropical climate. Temperatures are warm and rain falls all year.

> **What three regions make up the Pacific Islands?**
>
> _____
>
> _____
>
> _____

HISTORY AND CULTURE

People began settling the Pacific more than 40,000 years ago. They arrived in Melanesia first. Polynesia was the last region to be settled. Europeans first encountered the Pacific Islands in the 1500s. James Cook, a captain in the British navy, visited all the main regions in the 1700s. By the late 1800s Britain, Spain, France, and other European nations gained control of most of the islands. When the United States defeated Spain in the Spanish-American War, it took Guam as a **territory**, an area that is under the authority of another government. After World War I, Japan gained control of many islands. After World War II, the United Nations placed some islands under the control of the United States and its Allies.

More than 9 million people of many cultures and ethnic groups live in the Pacific Islands. Most are descended from the original settlers. Some are ethnic Europeans and Asians. Most islanders are now Christian. Many, however, continue to practice traditional customs, ranging from architecture to art styles and various ceremonies.

> Circle the name of the Pacific Island region that was first to be settled.

> About how many people live in the Pacific Islands?
> _____
> _____

THE PACIFIC ISLANDS TODAY

The Pacific Islands face important challenges today. They are trying to build stronger economies through tourism, agriculture, and fishing. Some countries, including Papua New Guinea, export gold, copper, and oil. The islands also must cope with the potentially damaging effects of past nuclear testing in the area and global warming.

> Underline three ways the Pacific Islands are trying to improve their economies.

CHALLENGE ACTIVITY

Critical Thinking: Drawing Conclusions Which island countries probably have stronger economies: those occupying high islands or those occupying low islands? Support your answer using details from the summary.